T0191054

The proceeds from the sale of this book will be used to support the mission of Library of America, a nonprofit organization that champions the nation's cultural heritage by publishing America's greatest writing in authoritative new editions and providing resources for readers to explore this rich, living legacy.

On Civil Disobedience

On Civil Disobedience

HENRY DAVID THOREAU

HANNAH ARENDT

Introduction by Roger Berkowitz

LIBRARY OF AMERICA

Contents

Introduction

by Roger Berkowitz

Henry David Thoreau never used the formulation "civil disobedience." As a practice, however, civil disobedience was first named and made part of our political vocabulary in 1866 when his essay "Resistance to Civil Government" (1849) was reprinted in a posthumous collection of his writings and given its now more familiar title. Perhaps no writer has made a more passionate, persuasive, and eloquent case for conscientious civil disobedience. There are some laws we disagree with and find offensive, but there are others so unjust that our continued obedience to our government implicates us in their wrong. Thoreau asks: "Must the citizen ever for a moment, or in the least degree, resign his conscience to the legislator?" And he answers definitively: No. The thoughtful and independent citizen must resist unjust laws. The radical insight that has made Thoreau's "Civil Disobedience" such a powerful inspiration for Leo Tolstoy, Mahatma Gandhi, and Martin Luther King Jr. is that since no government, even a democratic government, is based upon justice, each of us, to be free, thinking citizens, must live according to a higher law as we best understand it. Each of us has the right and indeed the *obligation* to refuse to support a government when it acts badly.

Thoreau begins his essay by writing, "I heartily accept the motto,—'That government is best which governs least.'" If this motto were carried out fully, he continues, it would mean, "'That government is best which governs not at all'; and when men are prepared for it, that will be the kind of government which they will have." It was James Madison who said, "If Men were angels, no government would be necessary."[1] Thoreau does not think men are angels, but he does believe in the ideal of true anarchism, at least as an aspiration that raises doubt about our allegiance to government: "But, to speak practically and as a citizen, unlike those who call themselves no-government men, I ask for, not at once no government, but *at once* a better government. . . . Can there not be a government in which majorities do not virtually decide right and wrong, but conscience?"

For Thoreau, the foundation of moral governance is self-governance in the most radical sense. Who but the individual can determine the nature of their obligations? Majority rule is still rule, and Thoreau argues that every man should aspire to follow his conscience above any outside rules, even the rule of a democratic government. When we cast a ballot, we vote for a principle that we believe is right, but at the same time, assert our willingness to recognize whatever principle—be it right or wrong—the majority favors. Political membership requires consent, but morality is binding above and apart from consent.[2]

Thoreau's politics find expression primarily in morally inspired resistance to government. He remains ready at any moment to withdraw his allegiance—tenuous as it is—from the State. Government, he reminds us repeatedly, is an *expedient*. What the conscientious citizen recognizes is never the authority of the government but only the good that it sometimes does. Government "can have no pure right over my person and property but what I concede to it." Through their undue respect for the law, "Even the well-disposed are daily made the agents of injustice." To be sure, there are many other, more pleasant pursuits than politics that Citizen Thoreau would rather engage in (among them huckleberrying, the activity that he runs off to upon his release from jail). "I came into this world, not chiefly to make this a good place to live in," he says, "but to live in it, be it good or bad." And since injustice will always be "part of the necessary friction of the machine of government," Thoreau counsels that for the most part one should be content to stand apart from the machine and "let it go: perchance it will wear smooth,—certainly the machine will wear out." Eventually, however, politics intrudes rudely on the domain of private life, requiring not just the attention but the *action* of the citizen: "If the injustice . . . is of such a nature that it requires you to be the agent of injustice to another, then, I say, *break the law*. Let your life be a counter friction to *stop* the machine" (italics mine).

Few political theorists have given Thoreau's essay serious attention. An exception in this regard is George Kateb. In an attentive reading of "Civil Disobedience," Kateb argues that Thoreau wishes to reconceive American democratic wildness—a cultural wildness that is a matter of historical record—and find other, better outlets for it.[3] Kateb defines wildness as "excess and extremism, especially in the forms of insatiability and transgressiveness."[4] American democracy cannot be understood, Kateb writes, without understanding American wildness. More particularly, he argues, Thoreau wishes to make individual conscience a *force* in American politics. The moral wildness of conscience must answer the majoritarian wildness of American government when it engages in wickedness. Conscience is a weapon to be used "against the criminal wildness of social groups, no better than bands and gangs, who enslave blacks, dispossess Native Americans, and manipulate the government into making war against Mexico in order to rob it of half its territory."[5] Thoreau's anarchic disposition—"an ingrained irreverence toward government as a contemptible and intrusive servant"—grows into moral outrage or horror when government behaves wickedly.[6]

In 1843, Thoreau stopped paying the Massachusetts

poll tax of nine shillings, and he continued to with-
hold payments until 1849, in a principled act of civil
resistance to a government that supported slavery and
had invaded Mexico in a war of expansion. (The Massachusetts poll tax was a head tax imposed on all men
from the ages of twenty-two to seventy.) The law, in
the form of Sam Staples, the Concord jailer and tax
collector, finally caught up with Thoreau in the summer of 1846. Staples took Thoreau into custody on an
evening in late July, after giving him ample opportunities to pay his taxes—and even offering to pay the
tax himself. Written partly to explain his actions to his
fellow townsmen, Thoreau's essay describes the night
he spent in jail. Thoreau bemoans the fact that "someone interfered, and paid the tax"—likely his aunt Maria
Thoreau bailed him out, although legend has it that it
was his friend Ralph Waldo Emerson. Thoreau does
not explain how he believes his poll tax was being used
to help subsidize slavery or the war in Mexico, but he
also tells us that such a precise accounting is irrelevant
in grave matters of conscience: "I do not care to trace
the course of my dollar, if I could, till it buys a man or
a musket . . . but I am concerned to trace the effects of
my allegiance."

When confronted with an unjust government that is
pro-war and pro-slavery, Thoreau writes in "Civil Disobedience," a conscientious individual has the obligation to withdraw their allegiance to that government:

"What I have to do is to see, at any rate, that I do not lend myself to the wrong which I condemn." He at least will not be made *an agent of injustice* by lending his allegiance and financial support to Massachusetts, which benefits economically from slavery, if only indirectly, and sends its sons to fight in an unjust war. He will not participate in systemic injustice. He therefore stops paying his poll tax and declares his disaffiliation from the State. His aim is not to overturn the government, but to assert his right as a free person, to conscientiously disobey otherwise legitimate laws: "I think that we should be men first, and subjects afterward." He goes yet further: "In fact, I quietly declare war with the State, after my fashion, though I will still make what use and get what advantage of her I can." Disobedience to an unjust law or policy is civil when it constitutes a refusal to obey the law in the name of doing what one knows to be right, or refusing to be part of a system that one knows to be unjust.

In breaking the law for moral reasons, the conscientious person must be willing to make self-sacrifices, and Thoreau does so, willingly accompanying his jailor to the town prison. As an individual, the civil disobedient must be "prepared to do justice to the slave and to Mexico, *cost what it may*." "If I have unjustly wrested a plank from a drowning man, I must restore it to him though I drown myself." Such sacrifice is "inconvenient," Thoreau acknowledges, citing the theologian

William Paley. "But he that would save his life, in such a case, shall lose it. This people must cease to hold slaves, and to make war on Mexico, though it cost them their existence as a people."

Going to prison for a just cause is not something to be feared. It is only within his prison cell, Thoreau tells his readers, that he feels truly free. Having formalized his separation from an unjust State, he hears as if for the first time the sounds of the village. "I did not for a moment feel confined," he says, "and the walls seemed a great waste of stone and mortar. . . . I could not but smile to see how industriously they locked the door on my meditations, which followed them out again without let or hindrance, and *they* were really all that was dangerous." In his prison cell, he also sees his neighbors more clearly, recognizing that they do not really propose to do right, unwilling as they are to assume risk to their person or property. The act of disobeying combined with the willingness to be punished and imprisoned is freeing insofar as it cleanses and purifies the civil disobedient.

It is important to underscore that Thoreau's act of civil disobedience is based neither on a strictly private understanding of morality nor on a sense of his own innate moral superiority. He does not embrace that kind of subjectivity. The ground of his refusal to pay his taxes is not merely that *he* believes slavery and the war in Mexico are wicked, but that they are great evils and that the majority of his fellow citizens—or at least a large minority—understand these are morally wrong but yet do nothing to stop them. There are many among his neighbors who call themselves Abolitionists. They speak and vote against slavery, but that is all. "Even voting *for the right is doing* nothing for it," Thoreau says. "It is only expressing feebly your desire that it should prevail." In voting they do not prove their character. Their "vote is of no more worth than that of any unprincipled foreigner or hireling native, who may have been bought."

Thoreau does not imagine that his own small act of civil disobedience will stop the war or end slavery. He does believe, however, that through his example of courage and self-sacrifice, meaningful change can be brought about. This is because conscientious action works upon the opinions of others. "Action from principle, the perception and the performance of right, changes things and relations; it is essentially *revolutionary*" (italics mine). Thoreau believes that if those who say that slavery is wrong and yet do nothing *see* someone else resisting the government and risking something for their conscience, then the few, followed by the many, will rouse themselves. "I know this well, that if one thousand, if one hundred, if ten men whom I could name,—if ten *honest* men only,—ay, if *one* honest man, in this State of Massachusetts, *ceasing to hold slaves,* were actually to withdraw from this copartnership, and be locked up in the county jail therefor, it would be the abolition of slavery in America." The power of civil disobedience, even by one person, is that it can inspire the conformist and sleeping others who agree with you to finally act on their consciences as well. "It matters not how small the beginning may seem to be," Thoreau counsels. An act "well done" will have lasting power. We must imagine Thoreau's disobedient "multiplied indefinitely," Kateb memorably puts it, "rather than associated with many others in a common course of action."[7] And so begins Thoreau's "peaceable revolution."

As much as Thoreau aims at a peaceful, civil, and nonviolent revolution, the wildness inherent in his account opens the door to violence, whether intended or not. That is perhaps inevitable. Strong passions will be aroused. Moral horror and outrage may "overwhelm the conscience," in Kateb's phrase, in some instances replacing it with fanaticism.[8] In his later writings on John Brown and his raid on Harpers Ferry, Thoreau's position evolves more clearly from conscientious politics to morally justifiable violence (the lesser evil principle). Speaking of Brown in his 1859 lecture "A Plea for Captain John Brown," he says: "It was his peculiar doctrine that a man has a perfect right to interfere by force with a slaveholder, in order to rescue the slave. I agree with him." He calls Brown a Transcendentalist, a hero, a man of both principles and action. In any case, though less explicitly in "Civil Disobedience," Thoreau seems to reserve the right to violent revolution when injustices have become truly "unendurable." "But even suppose blood should flow," he asks. "Is there not a sort of blood shed when the conscience is wounded?" It is true that the end of slavery could only be brought about, and was brought about, through great violence. Thoreau died on May 6, 1862, three years before the conclusion of the Civil War, which claimed perhaps as many as 850,000 American lives.

* * *

First published in Elizabeth Peabody's *Aesthetic Papers* in 1849, Thoreau's essay was barely noticed at the time. Not so in its long, vibrant afterlife. Thoreau's "Civil Disobedience" has had a profound influence on both our political discourse and the tradition of civil disobedience around the world. "[Thoreau's] ideas influenced me greatly," Mahatma Gandhi acknowledged. "I adopted some of them and recommended the study of Thoreau to all my friends who were helping me in the cause of Indian independence. Why, I actually took the name of my movement from Thoreau's essay."[9] Similarly, Martin Luther King Jr. saw Thoreau as an important influence for his nonviolent civil disobedience movement. He wrote: "During my student days I read Henry David Thoreau's essay 'On Civil Disobedience' for the first time. Here, in this courageous New Englander's refusal to pay his taxes and his choice of jail rather than support a war that would spread slavery's territory into Mexico, I made my first contact with the theory of nonviolent resistance. Fascinated by the idea of refusing to cooperate with an evil system, I was so deeply moved that I reread the work several times."[10]

Mahatma Gandhi and Martin Luther King Jr. took from Thoreau's essay a strong moral spur to politics. Gandhi took seriously the idea that disobedience must be civil. As the political theorist Uday Mehta argues, "for Gandhi, civility was a mode of individual comportment, which had the crucial feature of tying ethics to politics in a way that never allowed the latter to assume an independence of purpose and instrumentality." Gandhi required that his volunteers in the movement "must explain to the signatory the full significance of the word 'civilly.'" To be civil, disobedience must follow a vow and "a vow was thus an exacting commitment about how to behave. It involved an articulation of the self, through the very denial of choice." Gandhian civil disobedience differs from mere lawbreaking because "civility represented the ineradicable presence and challenge of the absolute in the midst of the everyday routines of life and struggle."[11] For Gandhi, as for Thoreau, civil disobedience is a moral act of the individual in accord with immutable principles.

After Martin Luther King Jr. was arrested for leading the protest march in Birmingham, Alabama, in 1963, he wrote his "Letter from Birmingham Jail," offering one of the greatest justifications for civil disobedience ever written, very much in Thoreau's spirit. Responding to eight white religious leaders who criticized King for breaking the laws against protesting, he asserts that there is a moral obligation to resist unjust laws:

> You express a great deal of anxiety over our willingness to break laws. This is certainly a legitimate concern. Since we so diligently urge people to obey the Supreme Court's decision of 1954 outlawing segregation in the public schools, at first glance it may seem rather paradoxical for us consciously to break laws. One may well ask: "How can you advocate breaking some laws and obeying others?" The answer lies in the fact that there are two types of laws: just and unjust. I would be the first to advocate obeying just laws. One has not only a legal but a moral responsibility to obey just laws. Conversely, one has a moral responsibility to disobey unjust laws. I would agree with St. Augustine that "an unjust law is no law at all."[12]

Gandhi and King owe much to Thoreau's moral approach that equates civil disobedience with the demands of conscience and the protection of the individual soul; however, the civil disobedience movements Gandhi and King birthed moved beyond Thoreau's idea

of civil disobedience as an individual act of conscientious resistance. Gandhi and King led movements that
mobilized millions in the struggle to upend unjust laws
and pursue political reform. These movements of civil
disobedience were political: They aimed to change the
world and actualize a more just democracy rather than
to free the individual from a necessarily unjust democratic state.

* * *

Hannah Arendt's essay "Civil Disobedience"
appeared in *The New Yorker* in 1970, during the
height of the antiwar movement and at the beginning
of the post–civil rights movement era. Born Jewish in
1906 in Germany, Arendt was arrested by the Nazis in
1933, fled to Paris, and ultimately emigrated to New
York City. She became a U.S. citizen in 1950. At the time
of the appearance of "Civil Disobedience," her books
The Origins of Totalitarianism, *The Human Condition,
Eichmann in Jerusalem,* and *On Revolution* had already
established her as the leading political thinker of the
twentieth century. In her essay, Arendt takes aim at
Thoreau and the tradition that associates civil disobedience with conscientious action. With one eye cast at
the political and social movements reshaping America,
Arendt argues that Thoreau's civil disobedient is really
a conscientious objector, not a member of a political
movement. His essay thus fails to help us make sense

of the public and collective nature of civil disobedience. Thoreau is, in Arendt's view, fundamentally *unpolitical*.

Underscoring the individual and moral nature of Thoreau's 1846 act of civil resistance, Arendt insists that civil disobedience is necessarily collective political dissent. It is a group phenomenon that publicizes widely shared minority opinions via extraordinary means to contest unjust acts by a ruling majority. "Civil disobedience," she writes, "arises when a significant number of citizens have become convinced either that the normal channels of change no longer function, and grievances will not be heard or acted upon, or that, on the contrary, the government is about to change and has embarked upon and persists in modes of action whose legality and constitutionality are open to grave doubt." Civil disobedients "are in fact organized minorities, bound together by common opinion, rather than by common interest, and the decision to take a stand against the government's policies even if they have reason to assume that these policies are backed by a majority." When, say, citizens gather to block access to abortion clinics or to shut down an intersection to protest laws banning abortion, the "concerted action" of civil disobedients "springs from an agreement with each other, and it is this agreement that lends credence and conviction to their opinion." In other words, civil disobedience is never the act of a lone individual but necessarily the actions of an organized group that aims to change laws or to prevent unconstitutional changes in the law.

Civil disobedience has come to play an outsized role in American politics as instances of extralegal and nonresponsive governments have become increasingly commonplace. Writing in 1970, Arendt could point to "seven years of an undeclared war in Vietnam; the growing influence of secret agencies on public affairs; open or thinly veiled threats to liberties guaranteed under the First Amendment; attempts to deprive the Senate of its constitutional powers, followed by the President's invasion of Cambodia in open disregard for the Constitution, which explicitly requires congressional approval for the beginning of a war." Today, we see similar failures of normal channels of legal and constitutional government. Black Lives Matter, for example, is a response to violent and prejudiced policing. There are also radical movements led by the Tea Party and Donald Trump on the right and Occupy Wall Street and anti-establishment figures like David Graeber and Catherine Liu on the left, all mobilizing against the legal and civil bureaucracies or the deep state that supports the U.S. political establishment.

Arendt saw the rise of governmental bureaucracy as one of the gravest threats to political freedom. She calls bureaucracy "the rule of nobody" and worries that bureaucratic government is an "invisible government" that disempowers citizens and makes democracy evermore precarious. So much of the anger and dissatisfaction with government today is traceable to what Arendt calls the disempowerment of self-government by citizens and the elevation of bureaucratic elites and experts to positions of power insulated from democratic control. It is this cordoning off of power from the citizens that, Arendt argues, makes the collective power mobilized by civil disobedience so necessary and important.

The contemporary upsurge in civil disobedience is a sign of what Arendt, following the Marxist tradition, calls a revolutionary situation. In times of crisis and amid the erosion of faith in the government's authority, caused by the government's increased inability to function, doubts arise about its legitimacy. Arendt takes it for granted, as she says elsewhere, that the "loss of power and authority by all the great powers is clearly visible, even though it is accompanied by an immense accumulation of the means of violence in the hands of the governments."[13] It may even be the case that the augmentation of the technological means of control by governments persuades leaders that they can persist longer in an illegitimate revolutionary situation. And they may not be wrong. Revolutionary situations rarely lead to revolution. More often they lead to counterrevolution, to the rise of a dictator, or, most frequently, to nothing at all.

If we are to respond productively to our revolutionary situation without violent revolution or demagogic dictatorship, we need to develop a political institution that can mobilize citizens and bring about political and social change, and that does so while remaining within the constitutional and legal frame of legitimate action. Arendt's answer is civil disobedience. Civil disobedience is just the kind of institution that can invigorate democracy by crystallizing and protecting minority rights and organized dissent while at the same time avoiding revolution, dictatorship, and violence. "Dissent implies consent," she memorably says, "and is the hallmark of free government; one who knows that he may dissent knows also that he somehow consents when he does not dissent."

In a modern era defined by change, Arendt understands civil disobedience to be a kind of ballast. Change may be a constant of the human condition, but the rate or "velocity" of change is not. As the rate of change increases, so too does the need for stability, and the laws in such times may appear as a force of resistance to change. Which is why, as the pace of social and political change accelerates, civil disobedience allows a constitutional government to "prove flexible enough to survive the onslaught of change without civil war and without revolution." The ability to bring about radical political change within a stable legal framework is an essential characteristic of civil disobedience.

* * *

Arendt wrote her remarks on "Civil Disobedience" in response to a symposium organized in 1970 by the Bar

Association of the City of New York, which addressed the question "Is the law dead?" Much of the symposium concerned the then pressing issues of rising crime and disobedience in the United States. One of the panels, led by Eugene V. Rostow, the undersecretary of state for political affairs, had asked, what is the "citizen's moral relation to the law in a society of consent?" Arendt's essay seeks to answer this question and to argue that civil disobedience not only *is* compatible with a society of laws, but also is an essential institution of constitutional government.

The starting point of Arendt's defense of civil disobedience is her insistence that it is not criminal. Whereas Thoreau and the tradition of conscientious civil disobedience believe that punishment for breaking the law is a sign of the civil disobedient's willingness to suffer for their moral action, Arendt believes that civil disobedients are political actors and should not be treated as criminals. Of course, both civil and criminal disobedience involve breaching the law. But unlike the common lawbreaker, Arendt argues, the civil disobedient does not seek to *hide* from the law. Rather, the civil disobedient breaks the law in "open defiance" of authority. This public quality allows civil disobedience to be recognized as compatible with law and American institutions of government. Civil disobedients are acting together—*breathing together*, Arendt says—in the spirit of the laws. As an example of civil disobedience,

Arendt offers the Freedom Riders, who rode buses and organized sit-ins in flagrant violation of laws enforcing segregation. Such acts of civil disobedience, intended for the public good, not private gain, would make no sense when hidden from view. The civil disobedient is not a criminal but a political actor, someone whose action springs from agreement with others that "lends credence and conviction to their opinion."

A second characteristic of civil disobedience is nonviolence. For Arendt, if and when civil disobedients resort to violence, they disqualify themselves as civil disobedients and justify the label "rebels," diminishing the potential political impact of their actions and undermining civil disobedience as an institution. And yet, the civil disobedient does share with the revolutionary the "wish 'to change the world.'" By acting nonviolently, the civil disobedient does not aim at revolution and "'accepts, while the revolutionary rejects, the frame of established authority and the general legitimacy of the system of laws.'"[14] (Arendt complicates this observation, asking whether Gandhi accepted "the 'frame of established authority,' which was British rule of India?") But a "generally accepted necessary characteristic of civil disobedience is nonviolence."

Arendt imagines civil disobedience to be a modern and specifically American form of the right to dissent. Civil disobedience, she argues, is a uniquely American invention that emerges in the United States "in

accordance with the *spirit* of its laws." Though it is a
global phenomenon, only America has a word for civil
disobedience, she adds, and, given its unique history,
"the American republic is the only government having
at least a chance to cope with it." The bond between civil
disobedience and the spirit of American law is held
together not by a theory but, rather, by the shared experiences of the colonists. In Arendt's telling, the spirit
of American law is *consent*. By consent, she does not
mean a social contract between a people and its government—something, she adds, that can be quickly dis-
missed as a fiction. Against the Hobbesian idea of the
social contract in which "every individual concludes an
agreement with the strictly secular authorities to insure
his safety"—what Arendt calls the "vertical version of
the social contract"—she argues that the American
political experiment was founded on the discovery of a
"horizontal" version of consent.

Horizontal consent has its roots in the "prerevolutionary experience" of early colonial Americans.
That experience is marked by "numerous covenants
and agreements, from the Mayflower Compact to the
establishment of the thirteen colonies." Signed in 1620
aboard the *Mayflower,* anchored off the coast of pres-
ent-day Massachusetts, the Mayflower Compact was a
declaration of self-rule agreed to by the Pilgrims and
the commoners who had sailed with them. These future
citizens from all social and economic classes arrogated

to themselves the right to govern themselves, demanding that their government be one of consent. Arendt expresses amazement at the astounding confidence these original settlers "had in their own power, granted and confirmed by no one and as yet unsupported by any means of violence, to combine themselves together into a 'civil Body Politick.'"[15] This new body politic was to be held together not by force, but simply by the faith each person had in the loyalty of each to their mutual promises. It was this actual experience of their joining together and constituting new governments—something repeated in every colony and in towns and cities across the North American continent—that, Arendt argues, was new and distinctly American. The American republic "rests on the power of the people."

The power to covenant existed prior to America. But the generative idea of power through mutual promises and compacts was most often fleeting; it may have flared into existence, but it was quickly and consistently extinguished as new centers of power claimed for themselves the sovereignty and the right to govern. But this is not what happened in the American Revolution, at least in the first 150 years of the republic, where the "new American experience and the new American concept of power" was elevated and incorporated into constitutions and institutions "designed explicitly to preserve it."[16] In *On Revolution*, in which Arendt examines horizontal consent at greater length, she argues that the experience of the freedom to act together in assemblies and mutual compacts opened the American colonists to a "new experience of power." The colonists had a history of acting in concert—to build roads and places of worship, found communities, and govern themselves. It is the "great good fortune of the American Revolution," she notes, that the colonies, prior to the Revolutionary War, "were organized in self-governing bodies."[17] When the American Revolution broke out and the authority of the English king was rejected, the American revolutionaries were not transported into anarchy. This is because the colonists were experienced with organized power in government bodies through constituent assemblies.

What so impresses Arendt is that, in the wake of the liberation from England, the American colonists immediately took to governing themselves in legislatures elected according to constitutional principles, "so that there existed no gap, no hiatus, hardly a breathing spell between the war of liberation, the fight for independence which was the condition for freedom, and the constitution of the new states."[18] Without missing a beat, the colonists made use of their experience in self-government to put new constitutions before the people of the various states for popular approval. Thus, the American constitutions were not simply acts of government designed to limit the government and protect civil liberties. Rather, the constitutions were active examples of a people coming together to constitute themselves. The American constitutions were more about creating *new* powers than about limiting power, and it was this task, "the creation of new power," that Arendt saw to be the central activity of the American Revolution.[19] The difference between American constitutions and their European descendants is that in America the constitutions were not made and imposed by experts but were constituted by the people themselves.

When Arendt published *On Revolution* in 1963, she worried that Americans had lost the foundation of their freedom and power, because the U.S. Constitution did not in the end institutionalize the public spaces of power that had given Americans the experience of freedom. There is no institutional space guaranteed by the Constitution for town hall meetings, citizen deliberation, or civic associations. Thomas Jefferson himself saw this problem and understood that while the Constitution "had given freedom to the people," it "had failed to provide a space where this freedom could be exercised."[20] For Arendt and for Jefferson, "the failure of the founders to incorporate the township and the town-hall meeting into the Constitution" meant that representation came to supplant the experience of freedom in self-government: "'the school of the people' [Emerson's phrase] in political matters had withered away."[21] And since the "Constitution itself provided a public space only for the representatives of the people, and not for the people themselves," the expected result was their increasing lethargy and "inattention to public business."[22] This failure to guarantee in the Constitution spaces of freedom for the people meant that the "treasure" of the American Revolution, the experience of freedom that underlay the foundation of freedom, was lost. Arendt's conclusion in *On Revolution* is that the tragic loss of the revolutionary spirit of freedom was the result of a turn away from civic republicanism toward bourgeois consumption.

However, by the time she published "Civil Disobedience," the civil rights movement, the voting rights movement, and the antiwar movement had convinced her that the loss of the American tradition of joining together to act politically was by no means a fait accompli. The 1960s provided ample evidence that "Americans still regard association as 'the only means they have for acting,' and rightly so." The old traditions by which Americans joined together to right wrongs and pursue collective interests against a recalcitrant majority proved themselves to be yet alive. In the era's many acts of civil disobedience Arendt found hope that there was still life force in the American tradition of civic republicanism.

Arendt saw the rise of civil disobedience as so many contemporary instances of what Alexis de Tocqueville called the American penchant for joining together in voluntary associations. In *Democracy in America*,

Tocqueville writes: "As soon as several of the inhabitants of the United States have taken up an opinion or a feeling which they wish to promote in the world, they look out for mutual assistance; and as soon as they have found one another out, they combine. *From that moment, they are no longer isolated men but a power seen from afar,* whose actions serve for an example and whose language is listened to."[23] Citizens coming together to organize and act to correct an injustice by the majority is what links civic associations and civil disobedience. Which is why Arendt can write that "it is my contention that civil disobedients are nothing but the latest form of voluntary association, and that they are thus quite in tune with the oldest traditions of the country." The centrality of civil disobedience to Arendt's understanding of American politics leads her to a stunning plea: "If there is anything that urgently requires a new constitutional amendment and is worth all the trouble that goes with it," it is a constitutional right to disobedience.

* * *

Arendt is keenly sensitive to the potential risks of enshrining civil disobedience in the Constitution, acknowledging that the dangers of civil disobedience are "elemental." Civil disobedience mobilizes everyday citizens against the power of the elites and amplifies the voices of the disenfranchised and outsiders. It gives to minorities an instrument of power that is usually enjoyed by majorities, experts, and elites. In this way, civil disobedience reflects the radical democratic power of the townships that Tocqueville understood would often oppose the more civilized rule of urban and national elites. Tocqueville saw the spirit of the United States in townships governed by farmers, teachers, and shop owners. The township includes the "coarser elements" of the population who resist the educated opinion of the experts and elite politicians. That is why township freedom is usually sacrificed to civilized centralized government. And yet, it is in the townships, Tocqueville argues, that one finds the true spirit of American democracy. Arendt says the same about civil disobedience. She is well aware that in elevating civil disobedience and giving it institutional and constitutional protection in the name of political freedom, we risk unleashing "evil demons."

Arendt's politics does not run away from the risk of contest and conflict. In her essay "Is America by Nature a Violent Society?" she writes, "it seems true that America, for historical, social and political reasons, is more likely to erupt into violence than most other civilized countries."[24] The American propensity toward violence coexists with the country's deep respect for law, and this paradoxical tension between violence and lawfulness is rooted in the American traditions of political activism, freedom of assembly, and civil disobedience, which, for Arendt, are "among the crucial, most cherished and, perhaps, most dangerous rights of American citizens."[25] Precisely because of our constitutionally guaranteed rights of assembly, speech, and activism, the United States is perennially threatened with disunity and fundamental dissent. "[E]very time Washington is unreceptive to the claims of a sufficiently large number of citizens," she says, "the danger of violence arises. Violence—to take the law into one's own hands—is perhaps more likely to be the consequence of frustrated power in America than in other countries."[26] Violence emerges as a real possibility at those moments when diverse constituencies feel themselves abandoned and disempowered.

In "Civil Disobedience," Arendt quotes John C. Calhoun's *Disquisition on Government*, readily acknowledging its troubling racist and proslavery arguments but conceding that the Southern statesman "was certainly right when he held that in questions of great national importance the 'concurrence or acquiescence of the various portions of the community' are a prerequisite of constitutional government." At the core of the American constitutional system is our belief that democratic majorities must also take account of minority opposition. What Calhoun calls "concurrent majorities" are those groups that, while in the minority, nevertheless represent meaningful countermajoritarian opinions that cannot safely and justly be ignored. Arendt's point is that "we are dealing here with organized minorities that are too important, not merely in numbers, but in *quality of opinion*, to be safely disregarded." In a constitutional system, all groups that feel strongly enough to engage in civil disobedience must be heard to protect against the "dangers of unbridled majority rule."

Civil disobedience is the kind of active citizenship that has brought about, and might again bring about, revolutionary change without civil war. Arendt's prime example is the civil rights movement. The Fourteenth and Fifteenth Amendments, guaranteeing Black Americans the rights and protections of citizens, were "meant to translate into constitutional terms the change that had come about as the result of the Civil War." But the South resisted that change and developed the system of Jim Crow laws that evaded racial equality through the implementation of the inherently unequal "separate but equal." The Fourteenth Amendment became activated by the Supreme Court only in the 1950s and '60s, and the "plain fact is that the court chose to do so only when civil rights movements that, as far as Southern laws were concerned, were clearly movements of civil disobedience had brought about a drastic change in the attitudes of both black and white citizens." For Arendt, civil disobedience has succeeded where the laws have previously failed, to bring "into the open the 'American dilemma' and, perhaps for the first time, forced upon the nation the recognition of the enormity of the crime, not just of slavery, but of chattel slavery." In Arendt's telling, after the Amendments failed to establish the promised revolutionary refounding of America, that revolution, to the extent that it happened, was brought about by civil disobedience.

If one were to identify a leader of the civil rights movement who aimed at politics in an Arendtian sense, it would have to be Bayard Rustin, one of the great if still-unsung heroes of the civil rights movement's strategy of civil disobedience.[27] A gay, communist, African American activist who believed passionately in a nonviolent revolution, Rustin was instrumental in organizing the 1963 "March on Washington for Jobs and Freedom," best remembered today for Martin Luther King Jr.'s stirring "I Have a Dream" speech. It was Rustin who traveled to Montgomery, Alabama, in 1956 to help organize the bus boycott; it was Rustin who introduced King to Gandhi's thinking on nonviolent resistance; it was Rustin who was the first—or one of the first—to expand the civil rights movement politically by demonstrating against nuclear testing in North Africa; and it was Rustin who conceived the idea for the Southern Leadership Conference, only to be forced to resign from the organization because of controversy over his sexual orientation.

In his seminal manifesto of 1965, "From Protest to Politics: The Future of the Civil Rights Movement," Rustin argues that the destruction of legal racism is only the first phase of the civil rights struggle. To bring about true civil rights, the movement would have to move beyond combating legal racism to bringing about full political equality: "The minute the movement faced this question, it was compelled to expand its vision beyond race relations to economic relations."[28] What this means is that the revolution in civil rights could no longer be a matter of protesting unjust laws; it must transform itself from a protest movement into a political movement; it must become, he argues, "a conscious bid for *political power*."[29]

About the second stage of the movement, he says: "I believe that the Negro's struggle for equality in America is essentially revolutionary. . . . the term revolutionary, as I am using it, does not connote violence; it refers to the qualitative transformation of fundamental institutions, more or less rapidly, to the point where the social and economic structure which they comprised can no longer be said to be the same."[30] The struggle for civil rights, Rustin claims, will not stop moving until either it has been utterly defeated or it has won substantial equality. In his words, civil rights can only be won when a revolution brings about full employment, the abolition of slums, the reconstruction of our educational system, and new definitions of work and leisure. He continues: "Adding up the cost of such programs, we can only conclude that we are talking about a refashioning of our political economy."[31] What Rustin calls a revolution, Hannah Arendt calls politics, and she names that revolutionary politics civil disobedience; for both Rustin and Arendt, civil disobedience is a revolutionary form of politics.

* * *

Thoreau's moral wildness and Arendt's revolutionary constitutionalism, for all their irreconcilable differences, come together around a deep suspicion of democratic majority rule. Both aim to mobilize protest as a way to protect against the tendency for democracies to be carried away by the tyranny of the majority as well as the apathy and corruption of the citizenry. Both are skeptical that voting is an adequate activity of democratic citizenship. Democracy, they each argue, requires of its citizens a more active engagement that demands that each citizen act in accord with republican virtue. Thoreau and Arendt both hold up civil disobedience as a way of inspiring in citizens the virtue necessary to resist the conformity and passivity of democratic majority rule.

------

1. James Madison, *Federalist* No. 51, in *The Federalist Papers*, ed. C. Rossiter (New York: New American Library, 1961), p. 322.
2. "Wildness and Conscience: Emerson and Thoreau," in George Kateb, *Patriotism and Other Mistakes* (New Haven: Yale University Press, 2006), p. 267.
3. Ibid., pp. 245–71.
4. Ibid., p. 247.

5. Ibid., p. 250.

6. Ibid., p. 253.

7. Ibid., p. 260.

8. Ibid.

9. Webb Miller, *I Found No Peace: The Journal of a Correspondent* (New York: Simon and Schuster, 1936), p. 238.

10. Martin Luther King Jr., *The Autobiography of Martin Luther King Jr.,* edited by Clayborne Carson (New York: Warner Books, 1998), p. 14.

11. "Putting Courage at the Center," in Uday Singh Mehta, *A Different Vision: Gandhi's Critique of Political Rationality* (Harvard University Press, forthcoming).

12. Martin Luther King Jr., "Letter from Birmingham Jail," in *American Democracy*, edited by Nicholas Lemann (New York: Library of America, 2020), p. 249.

13. "Thoughts on Politics and Revolution," in Hannah Arendt, *Crises of the Republic* (New York: Harcourt Brace Jovanovich, 1972), p. 205.

14. Here in her essay Arendt cites Carl Cohen.

15. Hannah Arendt, *On Revolution* (New York: Penguin, 1990), p. 167.

16. Ibid., pp. 166–67.

17. Ibid., p. 165.

18. Ibid., p. 141.

19. Ibid., p. 149.

20. Ibid., p. 235.

21. Ibid., pp. 235–36.

22. Ibid., p. 238.

23. Quoted in "Civil Disobedience" (emphasis added by Arendt).

24. "Is America by Nature a Violent Society?," in Hannah Arendt, *Thinking Without a Bannister*, ed. Jerome Kohn (New York: Schocken Books, 2018), p. 355.

25. Ibid., p. 356.

26. Ibid.

27. See Henry Louis Gates Jr., "Who Designed the March on Washington?," https://www.pbs.org/wnet/african-americans-many-rivers-to-cross/history/100-amazing-facts/who-designed-the-march-on-washington/

28. Bayard Rustin, "From Protest to Politics: The Future of the Civil Rights Movement," *Commentary* 39 (February 1965), p. 64.
29. Ibid.
30. Ibid., p. 65.
31. Ibid.

ON CIVIL DISOBEDIENCE

Henry David Thoreau
Civil Disobedience

I HEARTILY accept the motto,—"That government is best which governs least"; and I should like to see it acted up to more rapidly and systematically. Carried out, it finally amounts to this, which also I believe,— "That government is best which governs not at all"; and when men are prepared for it, that will be the kind of government which they will have. Government is at best but an expedient; but most governments are usually, and all governments are sometimes, inexpedient. The objections which have been brought against a standing army, and they are many and weighty, and deserve to prevail, may also at last be brought against a standing government. The standing army is only an arm of the standing government. The government itself, which is only the mode which the people have chosen to execute their will, is equally liable to be abused and perverted before the people can act through it. Witness the present Mexican war, the work of comparatively a few individuals using the standing government as their tool; for, in the outset, the people would not have consented to this measure.

This American government,—what is it but a tradition, though a recent one, endeavoring to transmit itself unimpaired to posterity, but each instant losing some of its integrity? It has not the vitality and force of a single living man; for a single man can bend it to his will. It is a sort of wooden gun to the people themselves. But it is not the less necessary for this; for the people must have some complicated machinery or other, and hear its din, to satisfy that idea of government which they have. Governments show thus how successfully men can be imposed on, even impose on themselves, for their own advantage. It is excellent, we must all allow. Yet this government never of itself furthered any enterprise, but by the alacrity with which it got out of its way. *It* does not keep the country free. *It* does not settle the West. *It* does not educate. The character inherent in the American people has done all that has been accomplished; and it would have done somewhat more, if the government had not sometimes got in its way. For government is an expedient by which men would fain succeed in letting one another alone; and, as has been said, when it is most expedient, the governed are most let alone by it. Trade and commerce, if they were not made of India-rubber, would never manage to bounce over the obstacles which legislators are continually putting in their way; and, if one were to judge these men wholly by the effects of their actions and not partly by their intentions, they would deserve to be classed and punished with those mischievous persons who put obstructions on the railroads.

But, to speak practically and as a citizen, unlike those who call themselves no-government men, I ask for, not at once no government, but *at once* a better government. Let every man make known what kind of government would command his respect, and that will be one step toward obtaining it.

After all, the practical reason why, when the power is once in the hands of the people, a majority are permitted, and for a long period continue, to rule, is not because they are most likely to be in the right, nor because this seems fairest to the minority, but because they are physically the strongest. But a government in which the majority rule in all cases cannot be based on justice, even as far as men understand it. Can there not be a government in which majorities do not virtually decide right and wrong, but conscience?—in which majorities decide only those questions to which the rule of expediency is applicable? Must the citizen ever for a moment, or in the least degree, resign his conscience to the legislator? Why has every man a conscience, then? I think that we should be men first, and subjects afterward. It is not desirable to cultivate a respect for the law, so much as for the right. The only obligation which I have a right to assume, is to do at any time what I think right. It is truly enough said, that a corporation has no conscience; but a corporation of conscientious men is a corporation *with* a conscience. Law never made men a whit more just; and, by means of their respect for it, even the well-disposed are daily made the agents of injustice. A common and natural result of an undue respect for law is, that you may see a file of soldiers, colonel, captain, corporal, privates, powder-monkeys, and all, marching in admirable order over hill and dale to the wars, against their wills, ay, against their common sense and consciences, which makes it very steep marching indeed, and produces a palpitation of the heart. They have no doubt that it is a damnable business in which they are concerned; they are all peaceably inclined. Now, what are they? Men at all? or small movable forts and magazines, at the service of some unscrupulous man in power? Visit the Navy-Yard, and behold a marine, such a man as an American government can make, or such as it can make a man with its black arts,—a mere shadow and reminiscence of humanity, a man laid out alive and standing, and already, as one may say, buried under arms with funeral accompaniments, though it may be,—

> "Not a drum was heard, not a funeral note,
>   As his corse to the rampart we hurried;
> Not a soldier discharged his farewell shot
>   O'er the grave where our hero we buried."

The mass of men serve the state thus, not as men mainly, but as machines, with their bodies. They are the standing army, and the militia, jailers, constables, posse comitatus, &c. In most cases there is no free exercise whatever of the judgment or of the moral sense; but they put themselves on a level with wood and earth and stones; and wooden men can perhaps be manufactured that will serve the purpose as well. Such command no more respect than men of straw or a lump of dirt. They have the same sort of worth only as horses and dogs. Yet such as these even are commonly esteemed good citizens. Others,—as most legislators, politicians, lawyers, ministers, and office-holders,—serve the state chiefly with their heads; and, as they rarely make any moral distinctions, they are as likely to serve the Devil, without *intending* it, as God. A very few, as heroes, patriots, martyrs, reformers in the great sense, and *men*, serve the state with their consciences also, and so necessarily resist it for the most part; and they are commonly treated as enemies by it. A wise man will only be useful as a man, and will not submit to be "clay," and "stop a hole to keep the wind away," but leave that office to his dust at least:—

"I am too high-born to be propertied
To be a secondary at control,
Or useful serving-man and instrument
To any sovereign state throughout the world."

He who gives himself entirely to his fellow-men appears to them useless and selfish; but he who gives himself partially to them is pronounced a benefactor and philanthropist.

How does it become a man to behave toward this American government to-day? I answer, that he cannot without disgrace be associated with it. I cannot for an instant recognize that political organization as *my* government which is the *slave's* government also.

All men recognize the right of revolution; that is, the right to refuse allegiance to, and to resist, the government, when its tyranny or its inefficiency are great and unendurable. But almost all say that such is not the case now. But such was the case, they think, in the Revolution of '75. If one were to tell me that this was a bad government because it taxed certain foreign commodities brought to its ports, it is most probable that I should not make an ado about it, for I can do without them. All machines have their friction; and possibly this does enough good to counterbalance the evil. At any rate, it is a great evil to make a stir about it. But when the friction comes to have its machine, and oppression and robbery are organized, I say, let us not have such a machine any longer. In other words, when a sixth of the population of a nation which has undertaken to be the refuge of liberty are slaves, and a whole country is unjustly overrun and conquered by a foreign army, and subjected to military law, I think that it is not too soon for honest men to rebel and revolutionize. What makes this duty the more urgent is the fact, that the country so overrun is not our own, but ours is the invading army.

Paley, a common authority with many on moral questions, in his chapter on the "Duty of Submission to Civil Government," resolves all civil obligation into expediency; and he proceeds to say, "that so long as the interest of the whole society requires it, that is, so long as the established government cannot be resisted or changed without public inconveniency, it is the will of God that the established government be obeyed, and no longer. . . . This principle being admitted, the justice of every particular case of resistance is reduced to a computation of the quantity of the danger and grievance on the one side, and of the probability and expense of redressing it on the other." Of this, he says, every man shall judge for himself. But Paley appears never to have contemplated those cases to which the rule of expediency does not apply, in which a people, as well as an individual, must do justice, cost what it may. If I have unjustly wrested a plank from a drowning man, I must restore it to him though I drown myself. This, according to Paley, would be inconvenient. But he that would save his life, in such a case, shall lose it. This people must cease to hold slaves, and to make war on Mexico, though it cost them their existence as a people.

In their practice, nations agree with Paley; but does any one think that Massachusetts does exactly what is right at the present crisis?

> "A drab of state, a cloth-o'-silver slut,
>   To have her train borne up, and her soul trail in
>   the dirt."

Practically speaking, the opponents to a reform in Massachusetts are not a hundred thousand politicians at the
South, but a hundred thousand merchants and farmers
here, who are more interested in commerce and agriculture than they are in humanity, and are not prepared
to do justice to the slave and to Mexico, *cost what it
may*. I quarrel not with far-off foes, but with those who,
near at home, co-operate with, and do the bidding of,
those far away, and without whom the latter would be
harmless. We are accustomed to say, that the mass of
men are unprepared; but improvement is slow, because
the few are not materially wiser or better than the many.
It is not so important that many should be as good as
you, as that there be some absolute goodness somewhere; for that will leaven the whole lump. There are
thousands who are *in opinion* opposed to slavery and
to the war, who yet in effect do nothing to put an end
to them; who, esteeming themselves children of Washington and Franklin, sit down with their hands in their
pockets, and say that they know not what to do, and do
nothing; who even postpone the question of freedom to
the question of free-trade, and quietly read the prices-
current along with the latest advices from Mexico, after
dinner, and, it may be, fall asleep over them both. What
is the price-current of an honest man and patriot today? They hesitate, and they regret, and sometimes they
petition; but they do nothing in earnest and with effect.
They will wait, well disposed, for others to remedy the

evil, that they may no longer have it to regret. At most, they give only a cheap vote, and a feeble countenance and God-speed, to the right, as it goes by them. There are nine hundred and ninety-nine patrons of virtue to one virtuous man. But it is easier to deal with the real possessor of a thing than with the temporary guardian of it.

All voting is a sort of gaming, like checkers or back-gammon, with a slight moral tinge to it, a playing with right and wrong, with moral questions; and betting naturally accompanies it. The character of the voters is not staked. I cast my vote, perchance, as I think right; but I am not vitally concerned that that right should prevail. I am willing to leave it to the majority. Its obligation, therefore, never exceeds that of expediency. Even voting *for the right* is *doing* nothing for it. It is only expressing to men feebly your desire that it should prevail. A wise man will not leave the right to the mercy of chance, nor wish it to prevail through the power of the majority. There is but little virtue in the action of masses of men. When the majority shall at length vote for the abolition of slavery, it will be because they are indifferent to slavery, or because there is but little slavery left to be abolished by their vote. *They* will then be the only slaves. Only *his* vote can hasten the abolition of slavery who asserts his own freedom by his vote.

I hear of a convention to be held at Baltimore, or elsewhere, for the selection of a candidate for the

Presidency, made up chiefly of editors, and men who are politicians by profession; but I think, what is it to any independent, intelligent, and respectable man what decision they may come to? Shall we not have the advantage of his wisdom and honesty, nevertheless? Can we not count upon some independent votes? Are there not many individuals in the country who do not attend conventions? But no: I find that the respectable man, so called, has immediately drifted from his position, and despairs of his country, when his country has more reason to despair of him. He forthwith adopts one of the candidates thus selected as the only *available* one, thus proving that he is himself *available* for any purposes of the demagogue. His vote is of no more worth than that of any unprincipled foreigner or hireling native, who may have been bought. O for a man who is a *man*, and, as my neighbor says, has a bone in his back which you cannot pass your hand through! Our statistics are at fault: the population has been returned too large. How many *men* are there to a square thousand miles in this country? Hardly one. Does not America offer any inducement for men to settle here? The American has dwindled into an Odd Fellow,—one who may be known by the development of his organ of gregariousness, and a manifest lack of intellect and cheerful self-reliance; whose first and chief concern, on coming into the world, is to see that the Almshouses are in good repair; and, before yet he has lawfully donned the virile garb, to collect a fund for the support of the widows and orphans that may be; who, in short, ventures to live only by the aid of the Mutual Insurance company, which has promised to bury him decently.

It is not a man's duty, as a matter of course, to devote himself to the eradication of any, even the most enormous wrong; he may still properly have other concerns to engage him; but it is his duty, at least, to wash his hands of it, and, if he gives it no thought longer, not to give it practically his support. If I devote myself to other pursuits and contemplations, I must first see, at least, that I do not pursue them sitting upon another man's shoulders. I must get off him first, that he may pursue his contemplations too. See what gross inconsistency is tolerated. I have heard some of my townsmen say, "I should like to have them order me out to help put down an insurrection of the slaves, or to march to Mexico;—see if I would go"; and yet these very men have each, directly by their allegiance, and so indirectly, at least, by their money, furnished a substitute. The soldier is applauded who refuses to serve in an unjust war by those who do not refuse to sustain the unjust government which makes the war; is applauded by those whose own act and authority he disregards and sets at naught; as if the State were penitent to that degree that it hired one to scourge it while it sinned, but not to that degree that it left off sinning for a moment. Thus, under the name of Order and Civil Government, we are all made at last to pay homage to and support our own meanness. After the first blush of sin comes its indifference; and from immoral it becomes, as it were, *un*moral, and not quite unnecessary to that life which we have made.

The broadest and most prevalent error requires the most disinterested virtue to sustain it. The slight reproach to which the virtue of patriotism is commonly liable, the noble are most likely to incur. Those who, while they disapprove of the character and measures of a government, yield to it their allegiance and support, are undoubtedly its most conscientious supporters, and so frequently the most serious obstacles to reform. Some are petitioning the State to dissolve the Union, to disregard the requisitions of the President. Why do they not dissolve it themselves,—the union between them-selves and the State,—and refuse to pay their quota into its treasury? Do not they stand in the same relation to the State, that the State does to the Union? And have not the same reasons prevented the State from resisting the Union, which have prevented them from resisting the State?

How can a man be satisfied to entertain an opinion merely, and enjoy *it*? Is there any enjoyment in it, if his opinion is that he is aggrieved? If you are cheated out of a single dollar by your neighbor, you do not rest satis-fied with knowing that you are cheated, or with saying that you are cheated, or even with petitioning him to pay you your due; but you take effectual steps at once to obtain the full amount, and see that you are never cheated again. Action from principle, the perception and the performance of right, changes things and relations; it is essentially revolutionary, and does not consist wholly with anything which was. It not only divides states and churches, it divides families; ay, it divides the *individual*, separating the diabolical in him from the divine.

Unjust laws exist: shall we be content to obey them, or shall we endeavor to amend them, and obey them until we have succeeded, or shall we transgress them at once? Men generally, under such a government as this, think that they ought to wait until they have persuaded the majority to alter them. They think that, if they should resist, the remedy would be worse than the evil. But it is the fault of the government itself that the remedy *is* worse than the evil. *It* makes it worse. Why is it not more apt to anticipate and provide for reform? Why does it not cherish its wise minority? Why does it cry and resist before it is hurt? Why does it not encourage its citizens to be on the alert to point out its faults, and *do* better than it would have them? Why does it always crucify Christ, and excommunicate Copernicus and Luther, and pronounce Washington and Franklin rebels?

One would think, that a deliberate and practical denial of its authority was the only offence never contemplated by government; else, why has it not assigned its definite, its suitable and proportionate penalty? If a man who has no property refuses but once to earn nine shillings for the State, he is put in prison for a period unlimited by any law that I know, and determined only by the discretion of those who placed him there; but if he should steal ninety times nine shillings from the State, he is soon permitted to go at large again.

If the injustice is part of the necessary friction of the machine of government, let it go, let it go: perchance it will wear smooth,—certainly the machine will wear out. If the injustice has a spring, or a pulley, or a rope, or a crank, exclusively for itself, then perhaps you may consider whether the remedy will not be worse than the evil; but if it is of such a nature that it requires you to be the agent of injustice to another, then, I say, break the law. Let your life be a counter friction to stop the machine. What I have to do is to see, at any rate, that I do not lend myself to the wrong which I condemn.

As for adopting the ways which the State has provided for remedying the evil, I know not of such ways. They take too much time, and a man's life will be gone. I have other affairs to attend to. I came into this world, not chiefly to make this a good place to live in, but to live in it, be it good or bad. A man has not everything to do, but something; and because he cannot do *everything*, it is not necessary that he should do *something* wrong. It is not my business to be petitioning the Governor or the Legislature any more than it is theirs to petition me;

and, if they should not hear my petition, what should I do then? But in this case the State has provided no way: its very Constitution is the evil. This may seem to be harsh and stubborn and unconciliatory; but it is to treat with the utmost kindness and consideration the only spirit that can appreciate or deserves it. So is all change for the better, like birth and death, which convulse the body.

I do not hesitate to say, that those who call themselves Abolitionists should at once effectually withdraw their support, both in person and property, from the government of Massachusetts, and not wait till they constitute a majority of one, before they suffer the right to prevail through them. I think that it is enough if they have God on their side, without waiting for that other one. Moreover, any man more right than his neighbors constitutes a majority of one already.

I meet this American government, or its representative, the State government, directly, and face to face, once a year—no more—in the person of its tax-gatherer; this is the only mode in which a man situated as I am necessarily meets it; and it then says distinctly, Recognize me; and the simplest, the most effectual, and, in the present posture of affairs, the indispensablest mode of treating with it on this head, of expressing your little satisfaction with and love for it, is to deny it then. My civil neighbor, the tax-gatherer, is the very man I have to deal with,—for it is, after all, with men and not with parchment that I quarrel,—and he has voluntarily chosen to be an agent of the government. How shall he ever know well what he is and does as an officer of the government, or as a man, until he is obliged to consider whether he shall treat me, his neighbor, for whom he has respect, as a neighbor and well-disposed man, or as a maniac and disturber of the peace, and see if he can get over this obstruction to his neighborliness without a ruder and more impetuous thought or speech corresponding with his action. I know this well, that if one thousand, if one hundred, if ten men whom I could name,—if ten *honest* men only,—ay, if *one* HONEST man, in this State of Massachusetts, *ceasing to hold slaves*, were actually to withdraw from this copartnership, and be locked up in the county jail therefor, it would be the abolition of slavery in America. For it matters not how small the beginning may seem to be: what is once well done is done forever. But we love better to talk about it: that we say is our mission. Reform keeps many scores of newspapers in its service, but not one man. If my esteemed neighbor, the State's ambassador, who will devote his days to the settlement of the question of human rights in the Council Chamber, instead of being threatened with the prisons of Carolina, were to sit down the prisoner of Massachusetts, that State which is so anxious to foist the sin of slavery upon her sister,—though at present she can discover only an act of inhospitality to be the ground of a quarrel with her,—the Legislature would not wholly waive the subject the following winter.

Under a government which imprisons any unjustly, the true place for a just man is also a prison. The proper place to-day, the only place which Massachusetts has provided for her freer and less desponding spirits, is in her prisons, to be put out and locked out of the State by her own act, as they have already put themselves out by their principles. It is there that the fugitive slave, and the Mexican prisoner on parole, and the Indian come to plead the wrongs of his race, should find them; on that separate, but more free and honorable ground, where the State places those who are not *with* her, but *against* her,—the only house in a slave State in which a free man can abide with honor. If any think that their influence would be lost there, and their voices no longer afflict the ear of the State, that they would not be as an enemy within its walls, they do not know by how much truth is stronger than error, nor how much more eloquently and effectively he can combat injustice who has experienced a little in his own person. Cast your whole vote, not a strip of paper merely, but your whole influence. A minority is powerless while it conforms to the majority; it is not even a minority then; but it is irresistible when it clogs by its whole weight. If the alternative is to keep all just men in prison, or give up war and slavery, the State will not hesitate which to choose. If a thousand men were not to pay their tax-bills this year, that would not be a violent and bloody measure, as it would be to pay them, and enable the State to commit violence and shed innocent blood. This is, in fact, the definition of a peaceable revolution, if any such is possible. If the tax-gatherer, or any other public officer, asks me, as one has done, "But what shall I do?" my answer is, "If you really wish to do anything, resign your office." When the subject has refused allegiance, and the officer has resigned his office, then the revolution is accomplished. But even suppose blood should flow. Is there not a sort of blood shed when the conscience is wounded? Through this wound a man's real manhood and immortality flow out, and he bleeds to an everlasting death. I see this blood flowing now.

I have contemplated the imprisonment of the offender, rather than the seizure of his goods,—though both will serve the same purpose,—because they who assert the purest right, and consequently are most dangerous to a corrupt State, commonly have not spent much time in accumulating property. To such the State renders comparatively small service, and a slight tax is wont to appear exorbitant, particularly if they are obliged to earn it by special labor with their hands. If there were one who lived wholly without the use of money, the State itself would hesitate to demand it of him. But the rich man,—not to make any invidious comparison,—is always sold to the institution which makes him rich. Absolutely speaking, the more money, the less virtue; for money comes between a man and his objects, and obtains them for him; and it was certainly no great virtue to obtain it. It puts to rest many questions which he would otherwise be taxed to answer; while the only new question which it puts is the hard but superfluous one, how to spend it. Thus his moral ground is taken from under his feet. The opportunities of living are diminished in proportion as what are called the "means" are increased. The best thing a man can do for his culture when he is rich is to endeavor to carry out those schemes which he entertained when he was poor. Christ answered the Herodians according to their condition. "Show me the tribute money," said he;—and one took a penny out of his pocket;—if you use money which has the image of Cæsar on it, and which he has made current and valuable, that is, *if you are men of the State*, and gladly enjoy the advantages of Cæsar's government, then pay him back some of his own when he demands it; "Render therefore to Cæsar that which is Cæsar's, and to God those things which are God's,"—leaving them no wiser than before as to which was which; for they did not wish to know.

When I converse with the freest of my neighbors, I perceive that, whatever they may say about the magnitude and seriousness of the question, and their regard for the public tranquillity, the long and the short of the matter is, that they cannot spare the protection of the existing government, and they dread the consequences to their property and families of disobedience to it. For my own part, I should not like to think that I ever rely on the protection of the State. But, if I deny the authority of the State when it presents its tax-bill, it will soon take and waste all my property, and so harass me and my children without end. This is hard. This makes it impossible for a man to live honestly, and at the same time comfortably, in outward respects. It will not be worth the while to accumulate property; that would be sure to go again. You must hire or squat somewhere, and raise but a small crop, and eat that soon. You must live within yourself, and depend upon yourself always tucked up and ready for a start, and not have many affairs. A man may grow rich in Turkey even, if he will be in all respects a good subject of the Turkish government. Confucius said: "If a state is governed by the principles of reason, poverty and misery are subjects of shame; if a state is not governed by the principles of reason, riches and honors are the subjects of shame." No: until I want the protection of Massachusetts to be extended to me in some distant Southern port, where my liberty is endangered, or until I am bent solely on building up an estate at home by peaceful enterprise, I can afford to refuse allegiance to Massachusetts, and her right to my property and life. It costs me less in every sense to incur the penalty of disobedience to the State, than it would to obey. I should feel as if I were worth less in that case.

Some years ago, the State met me in behalf of the Church, and commanded me to pay a certain sum toward the support of a clergyman whose preaching my father attended, but never I myself. "Pay," it said, "or be locked up in the jail." I declined to pay. But, unfortunately, another man saw fit to pay it. I did not see why the schoolmaster should be taxed to support the priest, and not the priest the schoolmaster; for I was not the State's schoolmaster, but I supported myself by voluntary subscription. I did not see why the lyceum should not present its tax-bill, and have the State to back its demand, as well as the Church. However, at the request of the selectmen, I condescended to make some such statement as this in writing:—"Know all men by these presents, that I, Henry Thoreau, do not wish to be regarded as a member of any incorporated society which I have not joined." This I gave to the town clerk; and he has it. The State, having thus learned that I did not wish to be regarded as a member of that church, has never made a like demand on me since; though it said that it must adhere to its original presumption that time. If I had known how to name them, I should then have signed off in detail from all the societies which I never signed on to; but I did not know where to find a complete list.

I have paid no poll-tax for six years. I was put into a jail once on this account, for one night; and, as I stood considering the walls of solid stone, two or three feet thick, the door of wood and iron, a foot thick, and the iron grating which strained the light, I could not help being struck with the foolishness of that institution which treated me as if I were mere flesh and blood and bones, to be locked up. I wondered that it should have concluded at length that this was the best use it could put me to, and had never thought to avail itself of my services in some way. I saw that, if there was a wall of stone between me and my townsmen, there was a still more difficult one to climb or break through, before they could get to be as free as I was. I did not for a moment feel confined, and the walls seemed a great waste of stone and mortar. I felt as if I alone of all my townsmen had paid my tax. They plainly did not know how to treat me, but behaved like persons who are underbred. In every threat and in every compliment there was a blunder; for they thought that my chief desire was to stand the other side of that stone wall. I could not but smile to see how industriously they locked the door on my meditations, which followed them out again without let or hindrance, and *they* were really all that was dangerous. As they could not reach me, they had resolved to punish my body; just as boys, if they cannot come at some person against whom they have a spite, will abuse his dog. I saw that the State was half-witted, that it was timid as a lone woman with her silver spoons, and that it did not know its friends from its foes, and I lost all my remaining respect for it, and pitied it.

Thus the State never intentionally confronts a man's sense, intellectual or moral, but only his body, his senses. It is not armed with superior wit or honesty, but with superior physical strength. I was not born to be forced. I will breathe after my own fashion. Let us see who is the strongest. What force has a multitude? They only can force me who obey a higher law than I. They force me to become like themselves. I do not hear of *men* being *forced* to live this way or that by masses of men. What sort of life were that to live? When I meet a government which says to me, "Your money or your life," why should I be in haste to give it my money? It may be in a great strait, and not know what to do: I cannot help that. It must help itself; do as I do. It is not worth the while to snivel about it. I am not responsible for the successful working of the machinery of society. I am not the son of the engineer. I perceive that, when an acorn and a chestnut fall side by side, the one does not remain inert to make way for the other, but both obey their own laws, and spring and grow and flourish as best they can, till one, perchance, overshadows and destroys the other. If a plant cannot live according to its nature, it dies; and so a man.

The night in prison was novel and interesting enough. The prisoners in their shirt-sleeves were enjoying a chat and the evening air in the doorway, when I entered. But the jailer said,

"Come, boys, it is time to lock up"; and so they dispersed, and I heard the sound of their steps returning into the hollow apartments. My room-mate was introduced to me by the jailer, as "a first-rate fellow and a clever man." When the door was locked, he showed me where to hang my hat, and how he managed matters there. The rooms were whitewashed once a month; and this one, at least, was the whitest, most simply furnished, and probably the neatest apartment in the town. He naturally wanted to know where I came from, and what brought me there; and, when I had told him, I asked him in my turn how he came there, presuming him to be an honest man, of course; and, as the world goes, I believe he was. "Why," said he, "they accuse me of burning a barn; but I never did it." As near as I could discover, he had probably gone to bed in a barn when drunk, and smoked his pipe there; and so a barn was burnt. He had the reputation of being a clever man, had been there some three months waiting for his trial to come on, and would have to wait as much longer; but he was quite domesticated and contented, since he got his board for nothing, and thought that he was well treated.

He occupied one window, and I the other; and I saw, that, if one stayed there long, his principal business would be to look out the window. I had soon read all the tracts that were left there, and examined where former prisoners had broken out, and where a grate had been sawed off, and heard the history of the various occupants of that room; for I found that even here there was a history and a gossip which never circulated beyond the walls of the jail. Probably this is the only house in the town where verses are composed, which are afterward printed in a circular form, but not published. I was shown quite a long list of verses which were composed by some young men who had been detected in an attempt to escape, who avenged themselves by singing them.

I pumped my fellow-prisoner as dry as I could, for fear I should never see him again; but at length he showed me which was my bed, and left me to blow out the lamp.

It was like travelling into a far country, such as I had never expected to behold, to lie there for one night. It seemed to me that I never had heard the town-clock strike before, nor the evening sounds of the village; for we slept with the windows open, which were inside the grating. It was to see my native village in the light of the Middle Ages, and our Concord was turned into a Rhine stream, and visions of knights and castles passed before me. They were the voices of old burghers that I heard in the streets. I was an involuntary spectator and auditor of whatever was done and said in the kitchen of the adjacent village-inn,—a wholly new and rare experience to me. It was a closer view of my native town. I was fairly inside of it. I never had seen its institutions before. This is one of its peculiar institutions; for it is a shire town. I began to comprehend what its inhabitants were about.

In the morning, our breakfasts were put through the hole in the door, in small oblong-square tin pans, made to fit, and holding a pint of chocolate, with brown bread, and an iron spoon. When they called for the vessels again, I was green enough to return what bread I had left; but my comrade seized it, and said that I should lay that up for lunch or dinner. Soon after he was let out to work at haying in a neighboring field, whither he went every day, and would not be back till noon; so he bade me good-day, saying that he doubted if he should see me again.

When I came out of prison,—for some one interfered, and paid that tax,—I did not perceive that great changes had taken place on the common, such as he observed who went in a youth, and emerged a tottering and gray-headed man; and yet a change had to my eyes come over the scene,—the town, and State, and country,—greater than any that mere time could effect. I saw yet more distinctly the State in which I lived. I saw to what extent the people among whom I lived could be trusted as good neighbors and friends; that their friendship was for summer weather only; that they did not greatly propose to do right; that they were a distinct race from me by their prejudices and superstitions, as the Chinamen and Malays are; that, in their sacrifices to humanity, they ran no risks, not even to their property; that, after all, they were not so noble but they treated the thief as he had treated them, and hoped, by a certain outward observance and a few prayers, and by walking in a particular straight though useless path from time to time, to save their souls. This may be to judge my neighbors harshly; for I believe that many of them are not aware that they have such an institution as the jail in their village.

It was formerly the custom in our village, when a poor debtor came out of jail, for his acquaintances to salute him, looking through their fingers, which were crossed to represent the grating of a jail window, "How do ye do?" My neighbors did not thus salute me, but first looked at me, and then at one another, as if I had returned from a long journey. I was put into jail as I was going to the shoemaker's to get a shoe which was mended. When I was let out the next morning, I proceeded to finish my errand, and having put on my mended shoe, joined a huckleberry party, who were impatient to put themselves under my conduct; and in half an hour,—for the horse was soon tackled,—was in the midst of a huckleberry field, on one of our highest hills, two miles off, and then the State was nowhere to be seen.

This is the whole history of "My Prisons."

I have never declined paying the highway tax, because I am as desirous of being a good neighbor as I am of being a bad subject; and, as for supporting schools, I am doing my part to educate my fellow-countrymen now. It is for no particular item in the tax-bill that I refuse to pay it. I simply wish to refuse allegiance to the State, to withdraw and stand aloof from it effectually. I do not care to trace the course of my dollar, if I could, till it buys a man or a musket to shoot one with,—the dollar is innocent,—but I am concerned to trace the effects of my allegiance. In fact, I quietly declare war with the State, after my fashion, though I will still make what use and get what advantage of her I can, as is usual in such cases.

If others pay the tax which is demanded of me, from a sympathy with the State, they do but what they have already done in their own case, or rather they abet injustice to a greater extent than the State requires. If they pay the tax from a mistaken interest in the individual taxed, to save his property, or prevent his going to jail, it is because they have not considered wisely how far they let their private feelings interfere with the public good.

This, then, is my position at present. But one cannot be too much on his guard in such a case, lest his action be biassed by obstinacy, or an undue regard for the opinions of men. Let him see that he does only what belongs to himself and to the hour.

I think sometimes, Why, this people mean well; they are only ignorant; they would do better if they knew how: why give your neighbors this pain to treat you as they are not inclined to? But I think again, this is no reason why I should do as they do, or permit others to suffer much greater pain of a different kind. Again, I sometimes say to myself, When many millions of men, without heat, without ill will, without personal feeling of any kind, demand of you a few shillings only, without the possibility, such is their constitution, of retracting or altering their present demand, and without the possibility, on your side, of appeal to any other millions, why expose yourself to this overwhelming brute force? You do not resist cold and hunger, the winds and the waves, thus obstinately; you quietly submit to a thousand similar necessities. You do not put your head into the fire. But just in proportion as I regard this as not wholly a brute force, but partly a human force, and consider that I have relations to those millions as to so many millions of men, and not of mere brute or inanimate things, I see that appeal is possible, first and instantaneously, from them to the Maker of them, and, secondly, from them to themselves. But, if I put my head deliberately into the fire, there is no appeal to fire or to the Maker of fire, and I have only myself to blame. If I could convince myself that I have any right to be satisfied with men as they are, and to treat them accordingly, and not according, in some respects, to my requisitions and expectations of what they and I ought to be, then, like a good Mussulman and fatalist, I should endeavor to be satisfied with things as they are, and say it is the will of God. And, above all, there is this difference between resisting this and a purely brute or natural force, that I can resist this with some effect; but I cannot expect, like Orpheus, to change the nature of the rocks and trees and beasts.

I do not wish to quarrel with any man or nation. I do not wish to split hairs, to make fine distinctions, or set myself up as better than my neighbors. I seek rather, I may say, even an excuse for conforming to the laws of the land. I am but too ready to conform to them. Indeed, I have reason to suspect myself on this head; and each year, as the tax-gatherer comes round, I find myself disposed to review the acts and position of the general and State governments, and the spirit of the people, to discover a pretext for conformity.

> "We must affect our country as our parents;
>   And if at any time we alienate
>   Our love or industry from doing it honor,
>   We must respect effects and teach the soul
>   Matter of conscience and religion,
>   And not desire of rule or benefit."

I believe that the State will soon be able to take all my work of this sort out of my hands, and then I shall be no better a patriot than my fellow-countrymen. Seen from a lower point of view, the Constitution, with all its faults, is very good; the law and the courts are very respectable; even this State and this American government are, in many respects, very admirable and rare things, to be thankful for, such as a great many have described them; but seen from a point of view a little higher, they are what I have described them; seen from a higher still, and the highest, who shall say what they are, or that they are worth looking at or thinking of at all?

However, the government does not concern me much, and I shall bestow the fewest possible thoughts on it. It is not many moments that I live under a government, even in this world. If a man is thought-free, fancy-free, imagination-free, that which *is not* never for a long time appearing *to be* to him, unwise rulers or reformers cannot fatally interrupt him.

I know that most men think differently from myself; but those whose lives are by profession devoted to the study of these or kindred subjects, content me as little as any. Statesmen and legislators, standing so completely within the institution, never distinctly and nakedly behold it. They speak of moving society, but have no resting-place without it. They may be men of a certain experience and discrimination, and have no doubt invented ingenious and even useful systems, for which we sincerely thank them; but all their wit and usefulness lie within certain not very wide limits. They are wont to forget that the world is not governed by policy and expediency. Webster never goes behind government, and so cannot speak with authority about it. His words are wisdom to those legislators who contemplate no essential reform in the existing government; but for thinkers, and those who legislate for all time, he never once glances at the subject. I know of those whose serene and wise speculations on this theme would soon reveal the limits of his mind's range and hospitality. Yet, compared with the cheap professions of most reformers, and the still cheaper wisdom and eloquence of politicians in general, his are almost the only sensible and valuable words, and we thank Heaven for him. Comparatively, he is always strong, original, and, above all, practical. Still his quality is not wisdom, but prudence.

The lawyer's truth is not Truth, but consistency, or a consistent expediency. Truth is always in harmony with herself, and is not concerned chiefly to reveal the justice that may consist with wrong-doing. He well deserves to be called, as he has been called, the Defender of the Constitution. There are really no blows to be given by him but defensive ones. He is not a leader, but a follower. His leaders are the men of '87. "I have never made an effort," he says, "and never propose to make an effort; I have never countenanced an effort, and never mean to countenance an effort, to disturb the arrangement as originally made, by which the various States came into the Union." Still thinking of the sanction which the Constitution gives to slavery, he says, "Because it was a part of the original compact,—let it stand." Notwithstanding his special acuteness and ability, he is unable to take a fact out of its merely political relations, and behold it as it lies absolutely to be disposed of by the intellect,—what, for instance, it behooves a man to do here in America to-day with regard to slavery,—but ventures, or is driven, to make some such desperate answer as the following, while professing to speak absolutely, and as a private man,—from which what new and singular code of social duties might be inferred? "The manner," says he, "in which the governments of those States where slavery exists are to regulate it, is for their own consideration, under their responsibility to their constituents, to the general laws of propriety, humanity, and justice, and to God. Associations formed elsewhere, springing from a feeling of humanity, or any other cause, have nothing whatever to do with it. They have never received any encouragement from me, and they never will."*

They who know of no purer sources of truth, who have traced up its stream no higher, stand, and wisely stand, by the Bible and the Constitution, and drink at it there with reverence and humility; but they who behold where it comes trickling into this lake or that pool, gird up their loins once more, and continue their pilgrimage toward its fountain-head.

No man with a genius for legislation has appeared in America. They are rare in the history of the world. There are orators, politicians, and eloquent men, by the thousand; but the speaker has not yet opened his mouth to speak, who is capable of settling the much-vexed questions of the day. We love eloquence for its own sake, and not for any truth which it may utter, or any heroism it may inspire. Our legislators have not yet learned the comparative value of free-trade and of freedom, of union, and of rectitude, to a nation. They have no genius or talent for comparatively humble questions of taxation and finance, commerce and manufactures and agriculture. If we were left solely to the wordy wit of legislators in Congress for our guidance, uncorrected

* These extracts have been inserted since the Lecture was read.

by the seasonable experience and the effectual com-
plaints of the people, America would not long retain
her rank among the nations. For eighteen hundred
years, though perchance I have no right to say it, the
New Testament has been written; yet where is the legislator who has wisdom and practical talent enough to
avail himself of the light which it sheds on the science
of legislation?

The authority of government, even such as I am willing to submit to,—for I will cheerfully obey those who
know and can do better than I, and in many things even
those who neither know nor can do so well,—is still an
impure one: to be strictly just, it must have the sanction
and consent of the governed. It can have no pure right
over my person and property but what I concede to it.
The progress from an absolute to a limited monarchy,
from a limited monarchy to a democracy, is a progress
toward a true respect for the individual. Even the Chi-
nese philosopher was wise enough to regard the individual as the basis of the empire. Is a democracy, such
as we know it, the last improvement possible in government? Is it not possible to take a step further towards
recognizing and organizing the rights of man? There
will never be a really free and enlightened State, until
the State comes to recognize the individual as a higher
and independent power, from which all its own power
and authority are derived, and treats him accordingly.
I please myself with imagining a State at last which can

afford to be just to all men, and to treat the individual with respect as a neighbor; which even would not think it inconsistent with its own repose, if a few were to live aloof from it, not meddling with it, nor embraced by it, who fulfilled all the duties of neighbors and fellow-men. A State which bore this kind of fruit, and suffered it to drop off as fast as it ripened, would prepare the way for a still more perfect and glorious State, which also I have imagined, but not yet anywhere seen.

Hannah Arendt
Civil Disobedience

IN THE SPRING of 1970, the Bar Association of the
City of New York celebrated its centennial with
a symposium on the rather dismal question "Is the
law dead?" It would be interesting to know what precisely inspired this cry of despair. Was it the disastrous
increase in crime in the streets or was it the farther-
reaching insight that "the enormity of evil expressed
in modern tyrannies has undermined any simple faith
in the central importance of fidelity to law" in addition
to "ample evidence that skillfully organized campaigns
of civil disobedience can be very effective in securing
desirable changes in the law"?[1] The topics, at any event,
on which participants were asked by Eugene V. Rostow
to prepare their papers clearly encouraged a somewhat
brighter outlook. One of them proposed a discussion
of "the citizen's moral relation to the law in a society of
consent," and the following remarks are in answer to
this. The literature on the subject relies to large extent
on two famous men in prison—Socrates, in Athens,
and Thoreau, in Concord. Their conduct is the joy of
jurists because it seems to prove that disobedience to

the law can be justified only if the lawbreaker is willing and even eager to accept punishment for his act.
There are few who would not agree with Senator Philip
A. Hart's position: "Any tolerance that I might feel
toward the disobeyer is dependent on his willingness
to accept whatever punishment the law might impose."[2]
This argument harks back to the popular understanding, and perhaps misunderstanding, of Socrates, but its
plausibility in this country seems to be greatly strength-
ened by "one of the most serious oddities of our law
[through which an individual] is encouraged or in
some sense compelled to establish a significant legal
right through a personal act of civil disobedience."[3] This
oddity has given rise to a strange and, as we shall see,
not altogether happy theoretical marriage of morality
and legality, conscience and the law of the land.

Because "our dual system of law permits the possibility that state law will be inconsistent with federal
law,"[4] the civil-rights movement in its early stages,
though clearly in disobedience to ordinances as well as
laws of the South, could indeed be understood to have
done no more than "to appeal, in our federal system,
over the head of the law and the authority of the state,
to the law and authority of the nation"; there was, we
are told—a hundred years of nonenforcement notwithstanding—"not the faintest real doubt that the [states']
ordinances were void under federal law" and that "the
defiance of the law was all on the other side."[5] At first

glance, the merits of this construction seem consider-able. The jurist's chief difficulty in construing a com-patibility of civil disobedience with the legal system of the country, namely, that "the law cannot justify the breaking of the law,"[6] seems ingeniously solved by the duality of American law and the identification of civil disobedience with the violation of a law for the purpose of testing its constitutionality. There is also the added advantage, or so it seems, that because of its dual system American law, in distinction from other legal systems, has found a nonfictitious, visible place for that "higher law" on which "in one form or another jurisprudence keeps insisting."[7]

It would require quite a bit of ingenuity to defend this doctrine on theoretical grounds: the situation of the man who tests the legitimacy of a law by break-ing it is "only marginally, if at all, one of civil disobe-dience";[8] and the disobeyer who acts on strong moral conviction and appeals to a "higher law" will find it rather strange if he is asked to recognize the various decisions of the Supreme Court over the centuries as inspired by that law above all laws whose chief charac-teristic is its immutability. On factual grounds, at any rate, the doctrine was refuted when the civil disobedi-ents of the civil-rights movement smoothly developed into the resisters of the antiwar movement who clearly disobeyed federal law, and this refutation became final when the Supreme Court refused to rule on the legality of the war in Vietnam because of "the political question doctrine," that is, precisely for the same reason that unconstitutional laws had been tolerated without the slightest impediment for such a long time.

Meanwhile, the number of civil disobedients or potential civil disobedients—that is, of people who volunteered for demonstration duty in Washington—has steadily increased, and with it the inclination of the government either to treat the protesters as common criminals or to demand the supreme proof of "self-sacrifice": the disobedient who has violated valid law should "welcome his punishment." (Harrop A. Freeman has nicely pointed to the absurdity of this demand from a lawyer's point of view: "No lawyer goes into court and says, 'Your Honor, this man wants to be punished.'"[9]) And the insistence on this unfortunate and inadequate alternative is perhaps only natural "in a period of turmoil," when "the distinction between such acts [in which an individual breaks the law in order to test its constitutionality] and ordinary violations becomes much more fragile," and when, not local laws, but "the national lawmaking power" is being challenged.[10]

Whatever the actual causes of the period of turmoil—and they are of course factual and political ones—the present confusion, polarization, and growing bitterness of our debates are also caused by a theoretical failure to come to terms with and to understand the true character of the phenomenon. Whenever the jurists attempt to justify the civil disobedient on moral and legal grounds, they construe his case in the image of either the conscientious objector or the man who tests the constitutionality of a statute. The trouble is that the situation of the civil disobedient bears no analogy to either for the simple reason that he never exists as a single individual; he can function and survive only as a member of a group. This is seldom admitted, and even in these rare instances only marginally mentioned; "civil disobedience practiced by a single individual is unlikely to have much effect. He will be regarded as an eccentric more interesting to observe than to suppress. Significant civil disobedience, therefore, will be practiced by a number of people who have a community of interest."[11] Yet one of the chief characteristics of the act itself—conspicuous already in the case of the Freedom Riders—namely, "indirect disobedience," where laws (for instance, traffic regulations) are violated that the disobedient regards as nonobjectionable in themselves in order to protest unjust ordinances or governmental policies and executive orders, presupposes a group action (imagine a single individual disregarding traffic laws!) and has rightly been called disobedience "in the strict sense."[12]

It is precisely this "indirect disobedience," which would make no sense whatsoever in the case of the conscientious objector or the man who breaks a specific law to test its constitutionality, that seems legally unjustifiable. Hence, we must distinguish between conscientious objectors and civil disobedients. The latter are in fact organized minorities, bound together by common opinion, rather than by common interest, and the decision to take a stand against the government's policies even if they have reason to assume that these policies are backed by a majority; their concerted action springs from an agreement with each other, and it is this agreement that lends credence and conviction to their opinion, no matter how they may originally have arrived at it. Arguments raised in defense of individual conscience or individual acts, that is, moral imperatives and appeals to a "higher law," be it secular or transcendent,[13] are inadequate when applied to civil disobedience; on this level, it will be not only "difficult," but impossible "to keep civil disobedience from being a philosophy of subjectivity . . . intensely and exclusively personal, so that any individual, for whatever reason, can disobey."[14]

I

T HE IMAGES of Socrates and Thoreau occur not
only in the literature on our subject, but also, and
more importantly, in the minds of the civil disobedients themselves. To those who were brought up in the
Western tradition of conscience—and who was not?—
it seems only natural to think of their agreement with
others as secondary to a solitary decision *in foro conscientiae*, as though what they had in common with
others was not an opinion or a judgment at all, but a
common conscience. And since the arguments used to
buttress this position are usually suggested by more or
less vague reminiscences of what Socrates or Thoreau
had to say about the "citizen's moral relation to the law,"
it may be best to begin these considerations with a brief
examination of what these two men actually had to say
on the matter.

As for Socrates, the decisive text is, of course, Plato's
Crito, and the arguments presented there are much less
unequivocal and certainly less useful for the demand
of cheerful submission to punishment than the legal
and philosophical textbooks tell us. There is first the
fact that Socrates, during his trial, never challenged the
laws themselves—only this particular miscarriage of

justice, which he spoke of as the "accident" (τύχη) that had befallen him. His personal misfortune did not entitle him to "break his contracts and agreements" with the laws; his quarrel was not with the laws, but with the judges. Moreover, as Socrates pointed out to Crito (who tried to persuade him to escape and go into exile), at the time of the trial the laws themselves had offered him this choice: "At that time you could have done with the state's consent what you are trying now to do without it. But then you gloried in being willing to die. You said that you preferred death to exile." We also know, from the *Apology*, that he had the option of desisting from his public examination of things, which doubtless spread uncertainty about established customs and beliefs, and that again he had preferred death, because "an unexamined life is not worth living." That is, Socrates would not have honored his own words if he had tried to escape; he would have undone all he had done during his trial—would have "confirmed the judges in their opinion, and made it seem that their verdict was a just one." He owed it *to himself*, as well as to the citizens he had addressed, to stay and die. "It is the payment of a debt of honor, the payment of a gentleman who has lost a wager and who pays because he cannot otherwise live with himself. There has indeed been a contract, and the notion of a contract pervades the latter half of the *Crito*, but . . . the contract which is binding is . . . *the commitment involved in the trial*" (my italics).[15]

Thoreau's case, though much less dramatic (he spent one night in jail for refusing to pay his poll tax to a government that permitted slavery, but he let his aunt pay it for him the next morning), seems at first glance more pertinent to our current debates, for, in contradistinction to Socrates, he protested against the injustice of the laws themselves. The trouble with this example is that in "On the Duty of Civil Disobedience," the famous essay that grew out of the incident and made the term "civil disobedience" part of our political vocabulary, he argued his case not on the ground of a *citizen's* moral relation to the law, but on the ground of individual conscience and conscience's moral obligation: "It is not a man's duty, as a matter of course, to devote himself to the eradication of any, even the most enormous, wrong; he may still properly have other concerns to engage him; but it is his duty, at least, to wash his hands of it, and, if he gives it no thought longer, not to give it practically his support." Thoreau did not pretend that a man's washing his hands of it would make the world better or that a man had any obligation to do so. He "came into this world not chiefly to make this a good place to live in, but to live in it, be it good or bad." Indeed, this is how we all come into the world—lucky if the world and the part of it we arrive in is a good place to live in at the time of our arrival, or at least a place where the wrongs committed are not "of such a nature that it requires you to be the agent of injustice to another." For only if this is the case, "then, I say, break the law." And Thoreau was right: individual conscience requires nothing more.[16]

Here, as elsewhere, conscience is unpolitical. It is not primarily interested in the world where the wrong is committed or in the consequences that the wrong will have for the future course of the world. It does not say, with Jefferson, "I tremble *for my country* when I reflect that God is just; that His justice cannot sleep forever,"[17] because it trembles for the individual self and its integrity. It can therefore be much more radical and say, with Thoreau, "This people must cease to hold slaves, and to make war on Mexico, *though it cost them their existence as a people*" (italics added), whereas for Lincoln "the paramount object," even in the struggle for the emancipation of the slaves, remained, as he wrote in 1862, "to save the Union, and . . . not either to save or destroy slavery."[18] This does not mean that Lincoln was unaware of "the monstrous injustice of slavery itself," as he had called it eight years earlier; it means that he was also aware of the distinction between his "official duty" and his "personal wish that all men everywhere could be free."[19] And this distinction, if one strips it of the always complex and equivocal historical circumstances, is ultimately the same as Machiavelli's when he said, "I love my native city more than my own soul."[20] The discrepancy between "official duty" and "personal wish" in Lincoln's case no more indicates a lack of moral commitment than the discrepancy between city and soul indicates that Machiavelli was an atheist and did not believe in eternal salvation and damnation.

This possible conflict between "the good man" and "the good citizen" (according to Aristotle, the good man could be a good citizen only in a good state; according to Kant, even "a race of devils" could solve successfully the problem of establishing a constitution, "if only they are intelligent"), between the individual self, with or without belief in an afterlife, and the member of the community, or, as we would say today, between morality and politics, is very old—older, even, than the word "conscience," which in its present connotation is of relatively recent origin. And almost equally old are the justifications for the position of either. Thoreau was consistent enough to recognize and admit that he was open to the charge of irresponsibility, the oldest charge against "the good man." He said explicitly that he was "not responsible for the successful working of the machinery of society," was "not the son of the engineer." The adage *Fiat justicia et pereat mundus* (Let justice be done even if the world perishes), which is usually invoked rhetorically against the defenders of absolute justice, often for the purpose of excusing wrongs and crimes, neatly expresses the gist of the dilemma.

However, the reason that "at the level of individual morality, the problem of disobedience to the law is wholly intractable"[21] is of still a different order. The counsels of conscience are not only unpolitical; they are always expressed in purely subjective statements. When Socrates stated that "it is better to suffer wrong than to do wrong," he clearly meant that it was better *for him*, just as it was better for him "to be in disagreement with multitudes than, being one, to be in disagreement with [himself]."[22] Politically, on the contrary, what counts is that a wrong has been done; to the law it is irrelevant who is better off as a result—the doer or the sufferer. Our legal codes distinguish between crimes in which indictment is mandatory, because the community as a whole has been violated, and offenses in which only doers and sufferers are involved, who may or may not want to sue. In the case of the former, the states of mind of those involved are irrelevant, except insofar as intent is part of the overt act, or mitigating circumstances are taken into account; it makes no difference whether the one who suffered is willing to forgive or the one who did is entirely unlikely to do it again.

In the *Gorgias*, Socrates does not address the citizens, as he does in the *Apology* and, in support of the *Apology*, in the *Crito*. Here Plato lets Socrates speak as the philosopher who has discovered that men have intercourse not only with their fellow men but also with themselves, and that the latter form of intercourse— my being with and by myself—prescribes certain rules for the former. These are the rules of conscience, and they are—like those Thoreau announced in his essay— entirely negative. They do not say what to do; they say

what not to do. They do not spell out certain principles for taking action; they lay down boundaries no act
should transgress. They say: Don't do wrong, for then
you will have to live together with a wrongdoer. Plato,
in the later dialogues (the *Sophist* and the *Theaetetus*),
elaborated on this Socratic intercourse of me with
myself and defined thinking as the soundless dialogue
between me and myself; existentially speaking, this
dialogue, like all dialogues, requires that the partners
be friends. The validity of the Socratic propositions
depends upon the kind of man who utters them and the
kind of man to whom they are addressed. They are self-
evident truths for man insofar as he is a thinking being;
to those who don't think, who don't have intercourse
with themselves, they are not self-evident, nor can
they be proved.[23] Those men—and they are the "multitudes"—can gain a proper interest in themselves only,
according to Plato, by believing in a mythical hereafter
with rewards and punishments.

Hence, the rules of conscience hinge on interest in
the self. They say: Beware of doing something that you
will not be able to live with. It is the same argument that
led to "Camus's . . . stress on the necessity of resistance
to injustice *for the resisting individual's own health and
welfare*" (my italics).[24] The political and legal trouble
with such justification is twofold. First, it cannot be
generalized; in order to keep its validity, it must remain
subjective. What I cannot live with may not bother

another man's conscience. The result is that conscience will stand against conscience. "If the decision to break the law really turned on individual conscience, it is hard to see in law how Dr. King is better off than Governor Ross Barnett, of Mississippi, who also believed deeply in his cause and was willing to go to jail."[25] The second, and perhaps even more serious, trouble is that conscience, if it is defined in secular terms, presupposes not only that man possesses the innate faculty of telling right from wrong, but also that man is interested in himself, for the obligation arises from this interest alone. And this kind of self-interest can hardly be taken for granted. Although we know that human beings are capable of thinking—of having intercourse with themselves—we do not know how many indulge in this rather profitless enterprise; all we can say is that the habit of thinking, of reflecting on what one is doing, is independent of the individual's social, educational, or intellectual standing. In this respect, as in so many others, "the good man" and "the good citizen" are by no means the same, and not only in the Aristotelian sense. Good men become manifest only in emergencies, when they suddenly appear, as if from nowhere, in all social strata. The good citizen, on the contrary, must be conspicuous; he can be studied, with the not so very comforting result that he turns out to belong to a small minority: he tends to be educated and a member of the upper social classes.[26]

This whole question of the political weight to be accorded moral decisions—decisions arrived at *in foro conscientiae*—has been greatly complicated by the originally religious and later secularized associations that the notion of conscience acquired under the influence of Christian philosophy. As we use the word today, in both moral and legal matters, conscience is supposed to be always present within us, as though it were identical with consciousness. (It is true that it took language a long time to distinguish between the two, and in some languages—French, for instance—the separation of conscience and consciousness has never taken place.) The voice of conscience was the voice of God, and announced the Divine Law, before it became the *lumen naturale* that informed men of a higher law. As the voice of God, it gave positive prescriptions whose validity rested on the command "Obey God rather than men"—a command that was objectively binding without any reference to human institutions and that could be turned, as in the Reformation, even against what was alleged to be the divinely inspired institution of the Church. To modern ears, this must sound like "self-certification," which "borders on blasphemy"—the presumptuous pretension that one knows the will of God and is sure of his eventual justification.[27] It did not sound that way to the believer in a creator God who has revealed Himself to the one creature He created in His own image. But the anarchic nature of divinely inspired consciences, so blatantly manifest in the beginnings of Christianity, cannot be denied.

The law, therefore—rather late, and by no means in all countries—recognized religiously inspired conscientious objectors but recognized them only when they appealed to a Divine Law that was also claimed by a recognized religious group, which could not well be ignored by a Christian community. The present deep crisis in the churches and the increasing number of objectors who claim no relation to any religious institution, whether or not they claim divinely informed consciences, have thus created great difficulties. These difficulties are not likely to be dissolved by substituting the submission to punishment for the appeal to a publicly recognized and religiously sanctioned higher law. "The idea that paying the penalty justifies breaking the law derives, not from Gandhi and the tradition of civil disobedience, but from Oliver Wendell Holmes and the tradition of legal realism. . . . This doctrine . . . is plainly absurd . . . in the area of criminal law. . . . It is mindless to suppose that murder, rape or arson would be justified if only one were willing to pay the penalty."[28] It is most unfortunate that, in the eyes of many, a "self-sacrificial element" is the best proof of "intensity of concern,"[29] of "the disobedient's seriousness and his fidelity to law,"[30] for single-minded fanaticism is usually the hallmark of the crackpot and, in any case, makes impossible a rational discussion of the issues at stake.

Moreover, the conscience of the believer who lis-
tens to and obeys the voice of God or the commands
of the *lumen naturale* is a far cry from the strictly secular conscience—this knowing, and speaking with,
myself, which, in Ciceronian language, better than a
thousand witnesses testifies to deeds that otherwise
may remain unknown forever. It is this conscience that
we find in such magnificence in *Richard III*. It does no
more than "fill a man full of obstacles"; it is not always
with him but awaits him when he is alone, and loses
its hold when midnight is over and he has rejoined the
company of his peers. Then only, when he is no longer by himself, will he say, "Conscience is but a word
that cowards use,/Devised at first to keep the strong in
awe." The fear of being alone and having to face oneself
can be a very effective dissuader from wrongdoing, but
this fear, by its very nature, is unpersuasive of others.
No doubt even this kind of conscientious objection
can become politically significant when a number of
consciences happen to coincide, and the conscientious
objectors decide to enter the market place and make
their voices heard in public. But then we are no longer
dealing with individuals, or with a phenomenon whose
criteria can be derived from Socrates or Thoreau. What
had been decided *in foro conscientiae* has now become
part of public opinion, and although this particular
group of civil disobedients may still claim the initial
validation—their consciences—they actually rely no

longer on themselves alone. In the market place, the fate of conscience is not much different from the fate of the philosopher's truth: it becomes an opinion, indistinguishable from other opinions. And the strength of opinion does not depend on conscience, but on the number of those with whom it is associated—"unanimous agreement that 'X' is an evil . . . adds credence to the belief that 'X' *is* an evil."[31]

II

Disobedience to the law, civil and criminal, has become a mass phenomenon in recent years, not only in America, but also in a great many other parts of the world. The defiance of established authority, religious and secular, social and political, as a world-wide phenomenon may well one day be accounted the outstanding event of the last decade. Indeed, "the laws seem to have lost their power."[32] Viewed from the outside and considered in historical perspective, no clearer writing on the wall—no more explicit sign of the inner instability and vulnerability of existing governments and legal systems—could be imagined. If history teaches anything about the causes of revolution—and history does not teach much, but still teaches considerably more than social-science theories—it is that a disintegration of political systems precedes revolutions, that the telling symptom of disintegration is a progressive erosion of governmental authority, and that this erosion is caused by the government's inability to function properly, from which spring the citizens' doubts about its legitimacy. This is what the Marxists used to call a "revolutionary situation"—which, of course, more often than not does not develop into a revolution.

In our context, the grave threat to the judicial system of the United States is a case in point. To lament "the cancerous growth of disobediences"[33] does not make much sense unless one recognizes that for many years now the law-enforcement agencies have been unable to enforce the statutes against drug traffic, mugging, and burglary. Considering that the chances that criminal offenders in these categories will never be detected at all are better than nine to one and that only one in a hundred will ever go to jail, there is every reason to be surprised that such crime is not worse than it is. (According to the 1967 report of the President's Commission on Law Enforcement and Administration of Justice, "well over half of all crimes are never reported to the police," and "of those which are, fewer than one-quarter are cleared by arrest. Nearly half of all arrests result in the dismissal of charges.")[34] It is as though we were engaged in a nationwide experiment to find out how many potential criminals—that is, people who are prevented from committing crimes only by the deterrent force of the law—actually exist in a given society. The results may not be encouraging to those who hold that all criminal impulses are aberrations—that is, are the impulses of mentally sick people acting under the compulsion of their illness. The simple and rather frightening truth is that under circumstances of legal and social permissiveness people will engage in the most outrageous criminal behavior who under normal circumstances perhaps dreamed of such crimes but never considered actually committing them.[35]

In today's society, neither potential lawbreakers (that is, nonprofessional and unorganized criminals) nor law-abiding citizens need elaborate studies to tell them that criminal acts will probably—which is to say, predictably—have no legal consequences whatsoever. We have learned, to our sorrow, that organized crime is less to be feared than nonprofessional hoodlums— who profit from opportunity—and their entirely justified "lack of concern about being punished"; and this state of affairs is neither altered nor clarified by research into the "public's confidence in American judicial process."[36] What we are up against is not the judicial process, but the simple fact that criminal acts usually have no legal consequences whatsoever; they are not followed by judicial process. On the other hand, one must ask what would happen if police power were restored to the reasonable point where from 60 to 70 per cent of all criminal offenses were properly cleared by arrest and properly judged. Is there any doubt that it would mean the collapse of the already disastrously overburdened courts and would have quite terrifying consequences for the just as badly overloaded prison system? What is so frightening in the present situation is not only the failure of police power per se, but also that to remedy this condition radically would spell disaster for these other, equally important branches of the judicial system.

The answer of the government to this, and to similarly obvious breakdowns of public services, has invariably been the creation of study commissions, whose fantastic proliferation in recent years has probably made the United States the most researched country on earth. No doubt the commissions, after spending much time and money in order to find out that "the poorer you are, the more likely you are to suffer from serious malnutrition" (a piece of wisdom that even made the New York *Times*'s "Quotation of the Day"),[37] often come up with reasonable recommendations. These, however, are seldom acted on, but, rather, are subjected to a new panel of researchers. What all the commissions have in common is a desperate attempt to find out something about the "deeper causes" of whatever the problem happens to be—especially if it is the problem of violence— and since "deeper" causes are, by definition, concealed, the final result of such team research is all too often nothing but hypothesis and undemonstrated theory. The net effect is that research has become a substitute for action, and the "deeper causes" are overgrowing the obvious ones, which are frequently so simple that no "serious" and "learned" person could be asked to give them any attention. To be sure, to find remedies for obvious shortcomings does not guarantee solution of

the problem; but to neglect them means that the problem will not even be properly defined.[38] Research has
become a technique of evasion, and this has surely not
helped the already undermined reputation of science.

Since disobedience and defiance of authority are such
a general mark of our time, it is tempting to view civil
disobedience as a mere special case. From the jurist's
viewpoint, the law is violated by the civil, no less than
the criminal, disobedient, and it is understandable that
people, especially if they happen to be lawyers, should
suspect that civil disobedience, precisely because it is
exerted in public, is at the root of the criminal variety[39]—all evidence and arguments to the contrary notwithstanding, for evidence "to demonstrate that acts of
civil disobedience . . . lead to . . . a propensity toward
crime" is not "insufficient" but simply nonexistent.[40]
Although it is true that radical movements and, certainly, revolutions attract criminal elements, it would
be neither correct nor wise to equate the two; criminals
are as dangerous to political movements as they are to
society as a whole. Moreover, while civil disobedience
may be considered an indication of a significant loss
of the law's authority (though it can hardly be seen as
its cause), criminal disobedience is nothing more than
the inevitable consequences of a disastrous erosion of
police competence and power. Proposals for probing
the "criminal mind," either with Rorschach tests or by
intelligence agents, sound sinister, but they, too, belong

among the techniques of evasion. An incessant flow of sophisticated hypotheses about the mind—this most elusive of man's properties—of the criminal submerges the solid fact that no one is able to catch his body, just as the hypothetical assumption of policemen's "*latent negative attitudes*" covers up their overt negative record in solving crimes.[41]

Civil disobedience arises when a significant number of citizens have become convinced either that the normal channels of change no longer function, and grievances will not be heard or acted upon, or that, on the contrary, the government is about to change and has embarked upon and persists in modes of action whose legality and constitutionality are open to grave doubt. Instances are numerous: seven years of an undeclared war in Vietnam; the growing influence of secret agencies on public affairs; open or thinly veiled threats to liberties guaranteed under the First Amendment; attempts to deprive the Senate of its constitutional powers, followed by the President's invasion of Cambodia in open disregard for the Constitution, which explicitly requires congressional approval for the beginning of a war; not to mention the Vice President's even more ominous reference to resisters and dissenters as "'vultures' . . . and 'parasites' [whom] we can afford to separate . . . from our society with no more regret than we should feel over discarding rotten apples from a barrel"—a reference that challenges not only the laws of the

United States, but every legal order.[42] In other words, civil disobedience can be tuned to necessary and desirable change or to necessary and desirable preservation or restoration of the *status quo*—the preservation of rights guaranteed under the First Amendment, or the restoration of the proper balance of power in the government, which is jeopardized by the executive branch as well as by the enormous growth of federal power at the expense of states' rights. In neither case can civil disobedience be equated with criminal disobedience.

There is all the difference in the world between the criminal's avoiding the public eye and the civil disobedient's taking the law into his own hands in open defiance. This distinction between an open violation of the law, performed in public, and a clandestine one is so glaringly obvious that it can be neglected only by prejudice or ill will. It is now recognized by all serious writers on the subject and clearly is the primary condition for all attempts that argue for the compatibility of civil disobedience with law and the American institutions of government. Moreover, the common lawbreaker, even if he belongs to a criminal organization, acts for his own benefit alone; he refuses to be overpowered by the consent of all others and will yield only to the violence of the law-enforcement agencies. The civil disobedient, though he is usually dissenting from a majority, acts in the name and for the sake of a group; he defies the law and the established authorities on the ground of basic dissent, and not because he as an individual wishes to make an exception for himself and to get away with it. If the group he belongs to is significant in numbers and standing, one is tempted to classify him as a member of one of John C. Calhoun's "concurrent majorities," that is, sections of the population that are unanimous in their dissent. The term, unfortunately, is tainted by proslavery and racist arguments, and in the *Disquisition on Government*, where it occurs, it covers only interests, not opinions and convictions, of minorities that feel threatened by "dominant majorities." The point, at any rate, is that we are dealing here with organized minorities that are too important, not merely in numbers, but in *quality of opinion*, to be safely disregarded. For Calhoun was certainly right when he held that in questions of great national importance the "concurrence or acquiescence of the various portions of the community" is a prerequisite of constitutional government.[43] To think of disobedient minorities as rebels and traitors is against the letter and spirit of a Constitution whose framers were especially sensitive to the dangers of unbridled majority rule.

Of all the means that civil disobedients may use in the course of persuasion and of the dramatization of issues, the only one that can justify their being called "rebels" is the means of violence. Hence, the second generally accepted necessary characteristic of civil disobedience is nonviolence, and it follows that "civil disobedience is not revolution. . . . The civil disobedient accepts, while the revolutionary rejects, the frame of established authority and the general legitimacy of the system of laws."[44] This second distinction between the revolutionary and the civil disobedient, so plausible at first glance, turns out to be more difficult to sustain than the distinction between civil disobedient and criminal. The civil disobedient shares with the revolutionary the wish "to change the world," and the changes he wishes to accomplish can be drastic indeed—as, for instance, in the case of Gandhi, who is always quoted as the great example, in this context, of nonviolence. (Did Gandhi accept the "frame of established authority," which was British rule of India? Did he respect the "general legitimacy of the system of laws" in the colony?)

"Things of this world are in so constant a flux that nothing remains long in the same state."[45] If this sentence, written by Locke about three hundred years ago, were uttered today, it would sound like the understatement of the century. Still, it may remind us that change is not a modern phenomenon, but is inherent in a world inhabited and established by human beings, who come into it, by birth, as strangers and newcomers (νέοι, the new ones, as the Greeks used to call the young), and depart from it just when they have acquired the experience and familiarity that may in certain rare cases enable them to be "wise" in the ways of the world. "Wise men" have played various and sometimes significant roles in human affairs, but the point is that they have always been old men, about to disappear from the world. Their wisdom, acquired in the proximity of departure, cannot rule a world exposed to the constant onslaught of the inexperience and "foolishness" of newcomers, and it is likely that without this interrelated condition of natality and mortality, which guarantees change and makes the rule of wisdom impossible, the human race would have become extinct long ago out of unbearable boredom.

Change is constant, inherent in the human condition, but the velocity of change is not. It varies greatly from country to country, from century to century. Compared with the coming and going of the generations, the flux of the world's things occurs so slowly that the world offers an almost stable habitat to those who come and stay and go. Or so it was for thousands of years—including the early centuries of the modern age, when first the notion of change for change's sake, under the name of progress, made its appearance. Ours is perhaps the first century in which the speed of change in the things of the world has outstripped the change of its inhabitants. (An alarming symptom of this turnabout is the steadily shrinking span of the generations. From the traditional standard of three or four generations to a century, which corresponded to a "natural" generation gap between fathers and sons, we have now come to the point where four or five years of difference in

age are sufficient to establish a gap between the generations.) But even under the extraordinary conditions
of the twentieth century, which make Marx's admonition to change the world sound like an exhortation to
carry coals to Newcastle, it can hardly be said that man's
appetite for change has canceled his need for stability. It
is well known that the most radical revolutionary will
become a conservative on the day after the revolution.
Obviously, neither man's capacity for change nor his
capacity for preservation is boundless, the former being
limited by the extension of the past into the present—
no man begins *ab ovo*—and the latter by the unpredict-
ability of the future. Man's urge for change and his need
for stability have always balanced and checked each
other, and our current vocabulary, which distinguishes
between two factions, the progressives and the conser-
vatives, indicates a state of affairs in which this balance
has been thrown out of order.

No civilization—the man-made artifact to house
successive generations—would ever have been possible without a framework of stability, to provide the
wherein for the flux of change. Foremost among the
stabilizing factors, more enduring than customs, manners, and traditions, are the legal systems that regulate
our life in the world and our daily affairs with each
other. This is the reason it is inevitable that law in a time
of rapid change will appear as "a restraining force, thus
a negative influence in a world which admires positive

action."[46] The variety of such systems is great, both in time and in space, but they all have one thing in common—the thing that justifies us in using the same word for phenomena as different as the Roman *lex*, the Greek νόμς, the Hebrew *torah*—and this is that they were designed to insure stability. (There is another general characteristic of the law: that it is not universally valid, but is either territorially bound or, as in the instance of Jewish law, ethnically restricted; but this does not concern us here. Where both characteristics, stability and limited validity, are absent—where the so-called "laws" of history or nature, for instance, as they are interpreted by the head of state, maintain a "legality" that can change from day to day and that claims validity for all mankind—we are in fact confronted with lawlessness, though not with anarchy, since order can be maintained by means of compulsive organization. The net result, at any rate, is criminalization of the whole governmental apparatus, as we know from totalitarian government.)

Because of the unprecedented rate of change in our time and because of the challenge that change poses to the legal order—from the side of the government, as we have seen, as well as from the side of disobedient citizens—it is now widely held that changes can be effected by law, as distinguished from the earlier notion that "legal action [that is, Supreme Court decisions] can influence ways of living."[47] Both opinions seem to me to be based on an error about what the law can achieve and what it cannot. The law can indeed stabilize and legalize change once it has occurred, but the change itself is always the result of extralegal action. To be sure, the Constitution itself offers a quasi-legal way to challenge the law by breaking it, but, quite apart from the question of whether or not such breaches are acts of disobedience, the Supreme Court has the right to choose among the cases brought before it, and this choice is inevitably influenced by public opinion. The bill recently passed in Massachusetts to force a test of the legality of the Vietnam war, which the Supreme Court refused to decide upon, is a case in point. Is it not obvious that this legal action—very significant indeed—was the result of the civil disobedience of draft resisters, and that its aim was to legalize servicemen's refusal of combat duty? The whole body of labor legislation—the right to collective bargaining, the right to organize and to strike—was preceded by decades of frequently violent disobedience of what ultimately proved to be obsolete laws.

The history of the Fourteenth Amendment perhaps offers an especially instructive example of the relation between law and change. It was meant to translate into constitutional terms the change that had come about as the result of the Civil War. This change was not accepted by the Southern states, with the result that the provisions for racial equality were not enforced for roughly a hundred years. An even more striking example of the inability of the law to enforce change, is, of course, the Eighteenth Amendment, concerning Prohibition, which had to be repealed because it proved to be unenforceable.[48] The Fourteenth Amendment, on the other hand, was finally enforced by the legal action of the Supreme Court, but, although one may argue that it had always been "the plain responsibility of the Supreme Court to cope with state laws that deny racial equality,"[49] the plain fact is that the court chose to do so only when civil-rights movements that, as far as Southern laws were concerned, were clearly movements of civil disobedience had brought about a drastic change in the attitudes of both black and white citizens. Not the law, but civil disobedience brought into the open the "American dilemma" and, perhaps for the first time, forced upon the nation the recognition of the enormity of the crime, not just of slavery, but of chattel slavery—"unique among all such systems known to civilization"[50]—the responsibility for which the people have inherited, together with so many blessings, from their forefathers.

III

THE PERSPECTIVE of very rapid change suggests that there is "every likelihood of a progressively expanding role for civil disobedience in . . . modern democracies."[51] If "civil disobedience is here to stay," as many have come to believe, the question of its compatibility with the law is of prime importance; the answer to it may well decide whether or not the institutions of liberty will prove flexible enough to survive the onslaught of change without civil war and without revolution. The literature on the subject is inclined to argue the case for civil disobedience on the rather narrow grounds of the First Amendment, admitting its need of being "expanded" and expressing the hope "that future Supreme Court decisions will establish a new theory as to [its] place."[52] But the First Amendment unequivocally defends only "the freedom of speech and of the press," whereas the extent to which "the right of the people peacefully to assemble and to petition the government for a redress of grievances" protects freedom of action is open to interpretation and controversy. According to Supreme Court decisions, "conduct under the First Amendment does not enjoy the same latitude as speech does," and "conduct, as opposed to speech, is [of course] endemic" to civil disobedience.[53]

However, what is basically at stake here is not whether, and to what extent, civil disobedience can be justified by the First Amendment, but, rather, with what *concept* of law it is compatible. I shall argue in what follows that although the phenomenon of civil disobedience is today a world-wide phenomenon and even though it has attracted the interest of jurisprudence and political science only recently in the United States, it still is primarily American in origin and substance; that no other country, and no other language, has even a word for it, and that the American republic is the only government having at least a chance to cope with it—not, perhaps, in accordance with the statutes, but in accordance with the *spirit* of its laws. The United States owes its origin to the American Revolution, and this revolution carried within it a new, never fully articulated concept of law, which was the result of no theory but had been formed by the extraordinary experiences of the early colonists. It would be an event of great significance to find a constitutional niche for civil disobedience—of no less significance, perhaps, than the event of the founding of the *constitutio libertatis*, nearly two hundred years ago.

The citizen's moral obligation to obey the laws has traditionally been derived from the assumption that he either consented to them or actually was his own legislator; that under the rule of law men are not subject to an alien will but obey only themselves—with the result, of course, that every person is at the same time his own master and his own slave, and that what is seen as the original conflict between the citizen, concerned with the public good, and the self, pursuing his private happiness, is internalized. This is in essence the Rousseauan-Kantian solution to the problem of obligation, and its defect, from my point of view, is that it turns again on conscience—on the relation between me and myself.[54] From the point of view of modern political science, the trouble lies in the fictitious origin of consent: "Many . . . write as if there were a social contract or some similar basis for political obligation to obey the majority's will," wherefore the argument usually preferred is: We in a democracy have to obey the law because we have the right to vote.[55] But it is precisely these voting rights, universal suffrage in free elections, as a sufficient basis for a democracy and for the claim of public freedom, that have come under attack.

Still, the proposition set forth by Eugene Rostow that what needs to be considered is "the citizen's moral obligation to the law *in a society of consent*" seems to me crucial. If Montesquieu was right—and I believe he was—that there is such a thing as "the spirit of the laws," which varies from country to country and is different in the various forms of government, then we may say that consent, not in the very old sense of mere acquiescence, with its distinction between rule over willing subjects and rule over unwilling ones, but in the sense of active support and continuing participation in all matters of public interest, is the spirit of American law. Theoretically, this consent has been construed to be the result of a social contract, which in its more common form— the contract between a people and its government—is indeed easy to denounce as mere fiction. However, the point is that it was no mere fiction in the American prerevolutionary experience, with its numerous covenants and agreements, from the Mayflower Compact to the establishment of the thirteen colonies as an entity. When Locke formulated his social-contract theory, which supposedly explained the aboriginal beginnings of civil society, he indicated in a side remark which model he actually had in mind: "In the beginning, all the world was America."[56]

In theory, the seventeenth century knew and combined under the name of "social contract" three altogether different kinds of such aboriginal agreements. There was, *first*, the example of the Biblical covenant, which was concluded between a people as a whole and its God, by virtue of which the people consented to obey whatever laws an all-powerful divinity might choose to reveal to it. Had this Puritan version of consent prevailed, it would, as John Cotton rightly remarked, have "set up Theocracy . . . as the best form of government."[57] There was, *second*, the Hobbesian variety, according to which every individual concludes an agreement with the strictly secular authorities to insure his safety, for the protection of which he relinquishes all rights and powers. I shall call this the vertical version of the social contract. It is, of course, inconsistent with the American understanding of government, because it claims for the government a monopoly of power for the benefit of all subjects, who themselves have neither rights nor powers as long as their physical safety is guaranteed; the American republic, in contrast, rests on the power of the people—the old Roman *potestas in populo*—and power granted to the authorities is delegated power, which can be revoked. There was, *third*, Locke's aboriginal social contract, which brought about not government but society—the word being understood in the sense of the Latin *societas*, an "alliance" between all individual members, who contract for their government after they have mutually bound themselves. I shall call this the horizontal version of the social contract. This contract limits the power of each individual member but leaves intact the power of society; society then establishes government "upon the plain ground of an original contract among independent individuals."[58]

All contracts, covenants, and agreements rest on mutuality, and the great advantage of the horizontal version of the social contract is that this mutuality binds each member to his fellow citizens. This is the only form of government in which people are bound together not through historical memories or ethnic homogeneity, as in the nation-state, and not through Hobbes's Leviathan, which "overawes them all" and thus unites them, but through the strength of mutual promises. In Locke's view, this meant that society remains intact even if "the government is dissolved" or breaks its agreement with society, developing into a tyranny. Once established, society, as long as it exists at all, can never be thrown back into the lawlessness and anarchy of the state of nature. In Locke's words, "the power that every individual gave the society, when he entered into it, can never revert to the individuals again, as long as the society lasts, but will always remain in the community."[59] This is indeed a new version of the old *potestas in populo*, for the consequence is that, in contrast to earlier theories of the right to resistance, whereby the people could act only "when their Chains are on," they now had the right, again in Locke's words, "to prevent" the chaining.[60] When the signers of the Declaration of Independence "mutually pledged" their lives, their fortunes, and their sacred honor, they were thinking in this vein of specifically American experiences as well as in terms of the generalization and conceptualization of these experiences by Locke.

Consent—meaning that voluntary membership must be assumed for every citizen in the community—is obviously (except in the case of naturalization) at least as open to the reproach of being a fiction as the aboriginal contract. The argument is correct legally and historically but not existentially and theoretically. Every man is born a member of a particular community and can survive only if he is welcomed and made at home within it. A kind of consent is implied in every newborn's factual situation; namely, a kind of conformity to the rules under which the great game of the world is played in the particular group to which he belongs by birth. We all live and survive by a kind of *tacit consent*, which, however, it would be difficult to call voluntary. How can we will what is there anyhow? We might call it voluntary, though, when the child happens to be born into a community in which dissent is also a legal and *de-facto* possibility once he has grown into a man. Dissent implies consent, and is the hallmark of free government; one who knows that he may dissent knows also that he somehow consents when he does not dissent.

Consent as it is implied in the right to dissent—the spirit of American law and the quintessence of American government—spells out and articulates the tacit consent given in exchange for the community's tacit welcome of new arrivals, of the inner immigration through which it constantly renews itself. Seen in this perspective, tacit consent is not a fiction; it is inherent in the human condition. However, the general tacit consent—the "tacit agreement, a sort of *consensus universalis*," as Tocqueville called it[61]—must be carefully distinguished from consent to specific laws or specific policies, which it does not cover even if they are the result of majority decisions.[62] It is often argued that the consent to the Constitution, the *consensus universalis*, implies consent to statutory laws as well, because in representative government the people have helped to make them. This consent, I think, is indeed entirely fictitious; under the present circumstances, at any rate, it has lost all plausibility. Representative government itself is in a crisis today, partly because it has lost, in the course of time, all institutions that permitted the citizens' actual participation, and partly because it is now gravely affected by the disease from which the party system suffers: bureaucratization and the two parties' tendency to represent nobody except the party machines.

At any rate, the current danger of rebellion in the United States arises not from dissent and resistance to particular laws, executive orders, and national policies, not even from denunciation of the "system" or the "establishment" with its familiar overtones of outrage at the low moral standards of those in high places and the protective atmosphere of connivance that surrounds them. What we are confronted with is a constitutional crisis of the first order, and this crisis has been effected by two very different factors whose unfortunate coincidence has resulted in the particular poignancy as well as general confusion of the situation. There are the frequent challenges to the Constitution by the administration, with the consequential loss of confidence in constitutional processes by the people, that is, the with-drawal of consent; and there has come into the open, at about the same time, the more radical unwillingness of certain sections of the population to recognize the *consensus universalis.*

Tocqueville predicted almost a hundred and fifty years ago that "the most formidable of all the ills that threaten the future of the Union arises," not from slav-ery, whose abolition he foresaw, but "from the presence of a black population upon its territory."[63] And the rea-son he could predict the future of Negroes and Indi-ans for more than a century ahead lies in the simple and frightening fact that these people had never been included in the original *consensus universalis* of the American republic. There was nothing in the Consti-tution or in the intent of the framers that could be so construed as to include the slave people in the origi-nal compact. Even those who pleaded eventual eman-cipation thought in terms of segregation of Negroes or, preferably, of deportation. This is true of Jeffer-son—"Nothing is more certain written in the book of fate than that these people are to be free; nor is it less certain that the two races, equally free, cannot live in the same government"—as it is true of Lincoln, who tried, as late as 1862, "when a deputation of colored men came to see [him] . . . to persuade them to set up a colony in Central America."[64] It was the tragedy of the abolitionist movement, which in its earlier stages had also proposed deportation and colonization (to Liberia), that it could appeal only to individual conscience, and neither to the law of the land nor to the opinion of the country. This may explain its strong general anti-institutional bias, its abstract morality, which condemned all institutions as evil because they tolerated the evil of slavery, and which certainly did not help in promoting those elementary measures of humane reform by which in all other countries the slaves were gradually emancipated into the free society.[65]

We know that this original crime could not be remedied by the Fourteenth and Fifteenth Amendments; on the contrary, the *tacit* exclusion from the *tacit* consensus was made more conspicuous by the inability or unwillingness of the federal government to enforce its own laws, and as time went by and wave after wave of immigrants came to the country, it was even more obvious that blacks, now free, and born and bred in the country, were the only ones for whom it was not true that, in Bancroft's words, "the welcome of the Commonwealth was as wide as sorrow."[66] We know the result, and we need not be surprised that the present belated attempts to welcome the Negro population explicitly into the otherwise tacit *consensus universalis* of the nation are not trusted. (An explicit constitutional amendment, addressed specifically to the Negro people of America, might have underlined the great change more dramatically for these people who had never

been welcome, assuring them of its finality. Supreme
Court decisions are constitutional interpretations, of
which the Dred Scott decision, which held, in 1857, that
"Negroes are not and cannot be citizens in the meaning of the federal Constitution," is one.[67] The failure of
Congress to propose such an amendment is striking in
the light of the overwhelming vote for a constitutional
amendment to cure the infinitely milder discrimina-
tory practices against women.) At any rate, attempts of
integration often are met by rebuffs from black organizations, while quite a number of their leaders care little
about the rules of nonviolence for civil disobedience
and, often, just as little about the issues at stake—the
Vietnam war, specific defects in our institutions—
because they are in open rebellion against all of them.
And although they have been able to attract to their
cause the extreme fringe of radical disobedience, which
without them would probably have withered away long
ago, their instinct tells them to disengage themselves
even from these supporters, who, their rebellious spirit
notwithstanding, were included in the original contract
out of which rose the tacit *consensus universalis.*

Consent, in the American understanding of the
term, relies on the horizontal version of the social contract, and not on majority decisions. (On the contrary,
much of the thinking of the framers of the Constitution
concerned safeguards for dissenting minorities.) The
moral content of this consent is like the moral content

of all agreements and contracts; it consists in the obligation to keep them. This obligation is inherent in all promises. Every organization of men, be it social or political, ultimately relies on man's capacity for making promises and keeping them. The only strictly moral duty of the citizen is this twofold willingness to give and keep reliable assurance as to his future conduct, which forms the prepolitical condition of all other, specifically political, virtues. Thoreau's often quoted statement "The only obligation which I have a right to assume is to do at any time what I think right" might well be varied to: The only obligation which I *as a citizen* have a right to assume is to make and to keep promises.

Promises are the uniquely human way of ordering the future, making it predictable and reliable to the extent that this is humanly possible. And since the predictability of the future can never be absolute, promises are qualified by two essential limitations. We are bound to keep our promises provided that no unexpected circumstances arise, and provided that the mutuality inherent in all promises is not broken. There exist a great number of circumstances that may cause a promise to be broken, the most important one in our context being the general circumstance of change. And violation of the inherent mutuality of promises can also be caused by many factors, the only relevant one in our context being the failure of the established authorities to keep to the original conditions. Examples of such failures have become only too numerous; there is the case of an "illegal and immoral war," the case of an increasingly impatient claim to power by the executive branch of government, the case of chronic deception, coupled with deliberate attacks on the freedoms guaranteed under the First Amendment, whose chief political function has always been to make *chronic* deception impossible; and there has been, last but not least, the case of violations (in the form of war-oriented or other government-directed research) of the specific trust of the universities that gave them protection against political interference and social pressure. As to the debates about the last, those who attack these misuses and those who defend them unfortunately incline to agree on the basically wrong premise that the universities are mere "mirrors for the larger society," an argument best answered by Edward H. Levi, the president of the University of Chicago: "It is sometimes said that society will achieve the kind of education it deserves. Heaven help us if this is so."[68]

"The spirit of the laws," as Montesquieu understood it, is the principle by which people living under a particular legal system act and are inspired to act. Consent, the spirit of American laws, is based on the notion of a mutually binding contract, which established first the individual colonies and then the union. A contract presupposes a plurality of at least two, and every association established and acting according to the principle of

consent, based on mutual promise, presupposes a plurality that does not dissolve but is shaped into the form
of a union—*e pluribus unum*. If the individual members of the community thus formed should choose not
to retain a restricted autonomy, if they should choose to
disappear into complete unity, such as the *union sacrée*
of the French nation, all talk about the citizen's *moral*
relation to the law would be mere rhetoric.

Consent and the right to dissent became the inspiring and organizing principles of action that taught the
inhabitants of this continent the "art of associating
together," from which sprang those voluntary associations whose role Tocqueville was the first to notice,
with amazement, admiration, and some misgiving; he
thought them the peculiar strength of the American
political system.[69] The few chapters he devoted to them
are still by far the best in the not very large literature
on the subject. The words with which he introduced
it—"In no country in the world has the principle of
association been more successfully used or applied to
a greater multitude of objects than in America"—are
no less true today than they were nearly a hundred
and fifty years ago; and neither is the conclusion that
"nothing . . . is more deserving of our attention than
the moral and intellectual associations of America."
Voluntary associations are not parties; they are *ad-hoc*
organizations that pursue short-term goals and disap-

pear when the goal has been reached. Only in the case
of their prolonged failure and of an aim of great importance may they "constitute, as it were, a separate nation
in the midst of the nation, a government within the
government." (This happened in 1861, about thirty years
after Tocqueville wrote these words, and it could happen again; the challenge of the Massachusetts legislature to the foreign policy of the administration is a clear
warning.) Alas, under the conditions of mass society,
especially in the big cities, it is no longer true that their
spirit "pervades every act of social life," and while this
may have resulted in a certain decline in the huge number of joiners in the population—of Babbitts, who are
the specifically American version of the Philistine—the
perhaps welcome refusal to form associations "for the
smallest undertakings" is paid for by an evident decline
in the appetite for action. For Americans still regard
association as "the only means they have for acting,"
and rightly so. The last few years, with the mass demonstrations in Washington, often organized on the spur of
the moment, have shown to what an unexpected extent
the old traditions are still alive. Tocqueville's account
could almost be written today: "As soon as several of
the inhabitants of the United States have taken up an
opinion or a feeling which they wish to promote in the
world," or have found some fault they wish to correct,
"they look out for mutual assistance, and as soon as they
have found one another out, they combine. *From that*

*moment, they are no longer isolated men but a power
seen from afar*, whose actions serve for an example and
whose language is listened to" (my italics).

It is my contention that civil disobedients are nothing but the latest form of voluntary association, and
that they are thus quite in tune with the oldest traditions of the country. What could better describe them
than Tocqueville's words "The citizens who form the
minority associate in order, first, to show their numer-
ical strength and so to diminish the moral power of
the majority"? To be sure, it has been a long time since
"moral and intellectual associations" could be found
among voluntary associations—which, on the contrary, seem to have been formed only for the protection
of special interests, of pressure groups and the lobbyists
who represented them in Washington. I do not doubt
that the dubious reputation of the lobbyists is deserved,
just as the dubious reputation of the politicians in this
country has frequently been amply deserved. However,
the fact is that the pressure groups are also voluntary
associations, and that they are recognized in Washington, where their influence is sufficiently great for
them to be called an "assistant government";[70] indeed,
the number of registered lobbyists exceeds by far the
number of congressmen.[71] This public recognition is no
small matter, for such "assistance" was no more fore-
seen in the Constitution and its First Amendment than
freedom of association as a form of political action.[72]

No doubt "the danger of civil disobedience is elemental,"[73] but it is not different from, nor is it greater than, the dangers inherent in the right to free association, and of these Tocqueville, his admiration notwithstanding, was not unaware. (John Stuart Mill, in his review of the first volume of *Democracy in America*, formulated the gist of Tocqueville's apprehension: "The capacity of coöperation for a common purpose, heretofore a monopolized instrument of power in the hands of the higher classes, is now a most formidable one in those of the lowest.")[74] Tocqueville knew that "the tyrannical control that these societies exercise is often far more insupportable than the authority possessed over society by the government which they attack." But he knew also that "the liberty of association has become a necessary guarantee against the tyranny of the majority," that "a dangerous expedient is used to obviate a still more formidable danger," and, finally, that "it is by the enjoyment of dangerous freedom that the Americans learn the art of rendering the dangers of freedom less formidable." In any event, "if men are to remain civilized or to become so, the art of associating together must grow and improve *in the same ratio in which the equality of conditions is increased*" (my italics).

We need not go into the old debates about the glories and the dangers of equality, the good and the evil of democracy, to understand that all evil demons could be let loose if the original contractual model of the

associations—mutual promises with the moral impera-
tive *pacta sunt servanda*—should be lost. Under today's
circumstances, this could happen if these groups, like
their counterparts in other countries, were to substitute ideological commitments, political or other, for
actual goals. When an association is no longer capable or willing to unite "into one channel the efforts of
divergent minds" (Tocqueville), it has lost its gift for
action. What threatens the student movement, the
chief civil-disobedience group of the moment, is not
just vandalism, violence, bad temper, and worse manners, but the growing infection of the movement with
ideologies (Maoism, Castroism, Stalinism, Marxism-
Leninism, and the like), which in fact split and dissolve
the association.

Civil disobedience and voluntary association are
phenomena practically unknown anywhere else. (The
political terminology that surrounds them yields only
with great difficulty to translation.) It has often been
said that the genius of the English people is to muddle
through and that the genius of the American people is
to disregard theoretical considerations in favor of prag-
matic experience and practical action. This is doubtful;
undeniable, however, is that the phenomenon of voluntary association has been neglected and that the notion
of civil disobedience has only recently received the
attention it deserves. In contrast to the conscientious
objector, the civil disobedient is a member of a group,

and this group, whether we like it or not, is formed in accordance with the same spirit that has informed voluntary associations. The greatest fallacy in the present debate seems to me the assumption that we are dealing with individuals, who pit themselves subjectively and conscientiously against the laws and customs of the community—an assumption that is shared by the defenders and the detractors of civil disobedience. The fact is that we are dealing with organized minorities, who stand against assumed inarticulate, though hardly "silent," majorities, and I think it is undeniable that these majorities have changed in mood and opinion to an astounding degree under the pressure of the minorities. In this respect, it has perhaps been unfortunate that our recent debates have been dominated largely by jurists—lawyers, judges, and other men of law—for they must find it particularly difficult to recognize the civil disobedient as a member of a group rather than to see him as an individual lawbreaker, and hence a potential defendant in court. It is, indeed, the grandeur of court procedure that it is concerned with meting out justice to an individual, and remains unconcerned with everything else—with the *Zeitgeist* or with opinions that the defendant may share with others and try to present in court. The only noncriminal lawbreaker the court recognizes is the conscientious objector, and the only group adherence it is aware of is called "conspiracy"—an utterly misleading charge in such cases, since conspiracy requires not only "breathing together" but secrecy, and civil disobedience occurs in public.

Although civil disobedience is compatible with the *spirit* of American laws, the difficulties of incorporating it into the American legal system and justifying it on purely legal grounds seem to be prohibitive. But these difficulties follow from the nature of the law in general, not from the special spirit of the American legal system. Obviously, "the law cannot justify the violation of the law," even if this violation aims at preventing the violation of another law.[75] It is an altogether different question whether it would not be possible to find a recognized niche for civil disobedience in our institutions of government. This political approach to the problem is strongly suggested by the Supreme Court's recent denial of certiorari to cases in which the government's "illegal and unconstitutional" acts with respect to the war in Vietnam were contested, because the court found that these cases involve the so-called "political question doctrine," according to which certain acts of the two other branches of government, the legislative and the executive, "are not reviewable in the courts. The precise status and nature of the doctrine are much in dispute," and the whole doctrine has been called "a smoldering volcano which may now be about to fulfill its long promise of erupting into flaming controversy,"[76] but there is little doubt about the nature of those acts on which the court will not rule and which therefore are left outside legal controls. These acts are characterized by their "momentousness"[77] and by "an unusual need for unquestioning adherence to a political decision already made."[78] Graham Hughes, to whose excellent examination of the political question doctrine I am greatly indebted, immediately adds that "these considerations . . . certainly seem to imply *inter arma silent leges* and cast doubt on the aphorism that it is a Constitution that is being expounded." In other words, the political doctrine is in fact that loophole through which the sovereignty principle and the reason of state doctrine are permitted to filter back, as it were, into a system of government which in principle denies them.[79] Whatever the theory, the facts of the matter suggest that precisely in crucial issues the Supreme Court has no more power than an international court: both are unable to enforce decisions that would hurt decisively the interests of sovereign states and both know that their authority depends on prudence, that is, on not raising issues or making decisions that cannot be enforced.

The establishment of civil disobedience among our political institutions might be the best possible remedy for this ultimate failure of judicial review. The first step would be to obtain the same recognition for the civil-disobedient minorities that is accorded the numerous special-interest groups (minority groups, by definition) in the country, and to deal with civil-disobedient groups in the same way as with pressure groups, which, through their representatives—that is, registered lobbyists—are permitted to influence and "assist" Congress by means of persuasion, qualified opinion, and the numbers of their constituents. These minorities of opinion would thus be able to establish themselves as a power that is not only "seen from afar" during demonstrations and other dramatizations of their viewpoint, but is always present and to be reckoned with in the daily business of government. The next step would be to admit publicly that the First Amendment neither in language nor in spirit covers the right of association as it is actually practiced in this country—this precious privilege whose exercise has in fact been (as Tocqueville noted) "incorporated with the manners and customs of the people" for centuries. If there is anything that urgently requires a new constitutional amendment and is worth all the trouble that goes with it, it is certainly this.

Perhaps an emergency was needed before we could find a home for civil disobedience, not only in our political language, but in our political system as well. An emergency is certainly at hand when the established institutions of a country fail to function properly and its authority loses its power, and it is such an emergency in the United States today that has changed voluntary association into civil disobedience and transformed dissent into resistance. It is common knowledge that this condition of latent or overt emergency prevails at present—and, indeed, has prevailed for some time—in large parts of the world; what is new is that this country is no longer an exception. Whether our form of government will survive this century is uncertain, but it is also uncertain that it will not. Wilson Carey McWilliams has wisely said, "When institutions fail, political society depends on men, and men are feeble reeds, prone to acquiesce in—if not to commit—iniquity."[80] Ever since the Mayflower Compact was drafted and signed under a different kind of emergency, voluntary associations have been the specifically American remedy for the failure of institutions, the unreliability of men, and the uncertain nature of the future. As distinguished from other countries, this republic, despite the great turmoil of change and of failure through which it is going at present, may still be in possession of its traditional instruments for facing the future with some measure of confidence.

---

1. See Graham Hughes, "Civil Disobedience and the Political Question Doctrine," in *New York University Law Review*, 43:2 (March, 1968).

2. In *To Establish Justice, to Insure Domestic Tranquility*, Final Report of the National Commission on the Causes and the Prevention of Violence, December, 1969, p. 108. For the use of Socrates and Thoreau in these discussions, see also Eugene V.

Rostow, "The Consent of the Governed," in *The Virginia Quarterly*, Autumn, 1968.

3. Thus Edward H. Levi in "The Crisis in the Nature of Law," in The Record of the Association of the Bar of the City of New York, March, 1970. Mr. Rostow, on the contrary, holds that "it is a common error to think of such breaches of the law as acts of disobedience to law" (*op. cit.*), and Wilson Carey McWilliams in one of the most interesting essays on the subject—"Civil Disobedience and Contemporary Constitutionalism," in *Comparative Politics*, vol. I, 1969—seems to agree by implication. Stressing that the court's "tasks depend, in part, on public action," he concludes: "The Court acts, in fact, to authorize disobedience to otherwise legitimate authority, and it depends on citizens who will take advantage of its authorizations" (p. 216). I fail to see how this can remedy Mr. Levi's "oddity"; the lawbreaking citizen who wishes to persuade the courts to pass on the constitutionality of some statute must be willing to pay the price like any other lawbreaker for the act—either until the court has decided the case or if it should decide against him.

4. Nicholas W. Puner, "Civil Disobedience: An Analysis and Rationale," in *New York University Law Review*, 43:714 (October, 1968).

5. Charles L. Black, "The Problem of the Compatibility of Civil Disobedience with American Institutions of Government," in *Texas Law Review*, 43:496 (March, 1965).

6. See, in the special issue of the *Rutgers Law Review* (vol. 21, Fall, 1966) on "Civil Disobedience and the Law," Carl Cohen, p. 8.

7. *Ibid.*, Harrop A. Freeman, p. 25.

8. See Graham Hughes, *op. cit.*, p. 4.

9. *Rutgers Law Review, op. cit.*, p. 26, where Freeman argues against the opinion of Carl Cohen: "Because the civil disobedient acts within a framework of laws whose legitimacy he accepts, this legal punishment is more than a possible consequence of his act—it is the natural and proper culmination of it.... He thereby demonstrates his willingness even to sacrifice himself in behalf of that cause" (*ibid.*, p. 6).

10. See Edward H. Levi, *op. cit.*, and Nicholas W. Puner, *op. cit.*, p. 702.

11. Nicholas W. Puner, *op. cit.*, p. 714.

12. Marshall Cohen, "Civil Disobedience in a Constitutional

Democracy," in *The Massachusetts Review*, 10:211–226, Spring, 1969.

13. Norman Cousins has set forth a series of steps in which the concept of a purely secular higher law would function:

"If there is a conflict between the security of the sovereign state and the security of the human commonwealth, the human commonwealth comes first.

"If there is a conflict between the well-being of the nation and the well-being of mankind, the well-being of mankind comes first.

"If there is a conflict between the needs of this generation and the needs of later generations, the needs of the later generations come first.

"If there is a conflict between the rights of the state and the rights of man, the rights of man come first. The state justifies its existence only as it serves and safeguards the rights of man.

"If there is a conflict between public edict and private conscience, private conscience comes first.

"If there is a conflict between the easy drift of prosperity and the ordeal of peace, the ordeal of peace comes first." (*A Matter of Life*, 1963, pp. 83–84; cited in *Rutgers Law Review, op. cit.*, p. 26.)

I find it rather difficult to be convinced of this understanding of higher law "in terms of first principles," as Cousins thinks of his enumeration.

14. Nicholas W. Puner, *op. cit.*, p. 708.

15. See N. A. Greenberg's excellent analysis, "Socrates' Choice in the *Crito*" (*Harvard Studies in Classical Philology*, vol. 70, no. 1, 1965), which proved that the *Crito* can be understood only if read in conjunction with the *Apology*.

16. All quotations are from Thoreau's "On the Duty of Civil Disobedience" (1849).

17. *Notes on the State of Virginia*, Query XVIII (1781–85).

18. In his famous letter to Horace Greeley, quoted here from Hans Morgenthau, *The Dilemmas of Politics*, Chicago, 1958, p. 80.

19. Quoted from Richard Hofstadter, *The American Political Tradition*, New York, 1948, p. 110.

20. Allan Gilbert, ed., *The Letters of Machiavelli*, New York, 1961, letter 225.

21. *To Establish Justice . . . , op. cit.*, p. 98.

22. *Gorgias*, 482 and 489.

23. This is made quite clear in the second book of the *Republic*, where Socrates' own pupils "can plead the cause of injustice most eloquently and still not be convinced themselves" (357–367). They are and remain convinced of justice as a self-evident truth, but Socrates' arguments are not convincing and they show that with this kind of reasoning the cause of injustice can just as well be "proved."

24. Quoted by Christian Bay, "Civil Disobedience," in the *International Encyclopedia of the Social Sciences*, 1968, II, 486.

25. *To Establish Justice . . . , op. cit.*, p. 99.

26. Wilson Carey McWilliams, *op. cit.*, p. 223.

27. Thus Leslie Dunbar, as quoted in "On Civil Disobedience in Recent American Democratic Thought," by Paul F. Power, in *The American Political Science Review*, March, 1970.

28. Marshall Cohen, *op. cit.*, p. 214.

29. Carl Cohen, *op. cit.*, p. 6.

30. Thus Marshall Cohen, *op. cit.*

31. Nicholas W. Puner, *op. cit.*, p. 714.

32. Wilson Carey McWilliams, *op. cit.*, p. 211.

33. *To Establish Justice . . . op. cit.*, p. 89.

34. *Law and Order Reconsidered*, Report of the Task Force on Law and Law Enforcement to the National Commission on the Causes and Prevention of Violence, n.d., p. 266.

35. Horrible examples of this truth were presented during the so-called "Auschwitz trial" in Germany, for whose proceedings see Bernd Naumann, *Auschwitz*, New York, 1966. The defendants were "a mere handful of intolerable cases," selected from about 2,000 S.S. men posted at the camp between 1940 and 1945. All of them were charged with murder, the only offense which in 1963, when the trial began, was not covered by the statute of limitations. Auschwitz was the camp of systematic extermination, but the atrocities almost all the accused had committed had nothing to do with the order for the "final solution"; their crimes were punishable under Nazi law, and in rare cases such perpetrators were actually punished by the Nazi government. These defendants had not been specially selected for duty at an extermination camp; they had come to Auschwitz for no other reason than that they were unfit for military service. Hardly any of them had a criminal record of any sort, and none of them

a record of sadism and murder. Before they had come to Auschwitz and during the eighteen years they had lived in postwar Germany, they had been respectable and respected citizens, undistinguishable from their neighbors.

36. The allusion is to the million-dollar grant made by the Ford Foundation "for studies of the public's confidence in the American judicial process," in contrast to the "survey of law-enforcement officials" by Fred P. Graham, of the New York *Times*, which, with no research team, came to the obvious conclusion "that the criminal's lack of concern about being punished is causing a major and immediate crisis." See Tom Wicker, "Crime and the Courts," in the New York *Times*, April 7, 1970.

37. On April 28, 1970.

38. There is, for example, the well-known over-researched fact that children in slum schools do not learn. Among the more obvious causes is the fact that many such children arrive at school without having had breakfast and are desperately hungry. There are a number of "deeper" causes for their failure to learn, and it is very uncertain that breakfast would help. What is not at all uncertain is that even a class of geniuses could not be taught if they happened to be hungry.

39. Justice Charles E. Whittaker, like many others in the profession, "attributes the crisis to ideas of civil disobedience." See Wilson Carey McWilliams, *op. cit.*, p. 211.

40. *To Establish Justice . . . , op. cit.*, p. 109.

41. *Law and Order Reconsidered, op. cit.*, p. 291.

42. *The New Yorker*'s many excellent comments on the administration's almost open contempt of this country's constitutional and legal order, in its "Talk of the Town" column, are especially recommended.

43. *A Disquisition on Government* (1853), New York, 1947, p. 67.

44. Carl Cohen, *op. cit.*, p. 3.

45. Locke, *The Second Treatise of Government*, No. 157.

46. Edward H. Levi, *op. cit.*

47. J. D. Hyman, "Segregation and the Fourteenth Amendment," in *Essays in Constitutional Law*, Robert G. McCloskey, ed., New York, 1957, p. 379.

48. The widespread disobedience of the Prohibition amendment has, however, "no rightful claim to be called disobedience,"

because it was not practiced in public. See Nicholas W. Puner, *op. cit.*, p. 653.

49. Robert G. McCloskey in *op. cit.*, p. 352.

50. On this important point, which explains why emancipation had such disastrous consequences in the United States, see the splendid study *Slavery* by Stanley M. Elkins, New York, 1959.

51. Christian Bay, *op. cit.*, p. 483.

52. Harrop A. Freeman, *op. cit.*, p. 23.

53. Nicholas W. Puner, *op. cit.*, p. 694. For the meaning of the First Amendment's guarantee, see especially Edward S. Corwin, *The Constitution and What It Means Today*, Princeton, 1958. As to the question to what extent freedom of action is protected by the First Amendment, Corwin points out: "Historically, the right of petition is a primary right, the right peaceably to assemble a subordinate and instrumental right. . . . Today, however, the right of peaceable assembly is '. . . cognate to those of free speech and free press and is equally fundamental. . . . The holding of meetings for peaceable political action cannot be proscribed. These who assist in the conduct of such meetings cannot be branded as criminals on that score'" (pp. 203–204).

54. Another important defect has been pointed out by Hegel: "To be one's own master and servant seems to be better than to be somebody else's servant. However, the relation between freedom and nature, if . . . nature is being oppressed by one's own self, is much more artificial than the relation in natural law, according to which the domineering and commanding part is outside the living individual. In the latter case, the individual as a living entity retains its autonomous identity. . . . It is opposed by an alien power. . . . [Otherwise] its inner harmony is destroyed." In *Differenz des Fichte'schen und Schelling'schen Systems der Philosophie* (1801), Felix Meiner edition, p. 70.

55. Christian Bay, *op. cit.*, p. 483.

56. *Op. cit.*, No. 49.

57. See my discussion of Puritanism and its influence on the American Revolution in *On Revolution*, New York, 1963, pp. 171ff.

58. John Adams, *Novanglus. Works*, Boston, 1851, vol. IV, p. 110.

59. *Op. cit.*, No. 220.

60. *Ibid.*, No. 243.

61. "The republican government exists in America, without contention or opposition, without proofs or arguments, by a tacit

agreement, a sort of *consensus universalis*." *Democracy in America*, New York, 1945, vol. I, p. 419.

62. For the importance of this distinction, see Hans Morgenthau, *Truth and Power*, 1970, pp. 19ff.; and *The New Republic*, January 22, 1966, pp. 16–18.

63. *Op. cit.*, p. 356.

64. Hofstadter, *op. cit.*, p. 130.

65. Elkins, in Part IV of his book noted earlier, gives an excellent analysis of the sterility of the abolitionist movement.

66. See George Bancroft, *The History of the United States*, abridged edition by Russell B. Nye, Chicago, 1966, p. 44.

67. The case of *Dred Scott* v. *Sandford* came on appeal before the Supreme Court. Scott, a slave from Missouri, had been taken by his owner to Illinois and other territory where slavery was outlawed. Back in Missouri, Scott sued his owner, "arguing that these journeys to free areas had made him a free man." The court decided that Scott could "not bring suit in federal courts . . . because Negroes are not and cannot be citizens in the meaning of the federal Constitution." See Robert McCloskey, *The American Supreme Court*, Chicago, 1966, pp. 93–95.

68. *Point of View. Talks on Education*, Chicago, 1969, pp. 139 and 170.

69. All the following citations of Tocqueville are from *op. cit.*, vol. I, chap. 12, and vol. II, book ii, chap. 5.

70. See Carl Joachim Friedrich, *Constitutional Government and Democracy*, Boston, 1950, p. 464.

71. Edward S. Corwin, *loc. cit.*

72. I do not doubt that "civil disobedience is a proper procedure to bring a law, believed to be unjust or invalid, into court or before the bar of public opinion." The question is only ". . . if this is indeed one of the rights recognized by the First Amendment," in the words of Harrop A. Freeman, *op. cit.*, p. 25.

73. Nicholas W. Puner, *op. cit.*, p. 707.

74. Reprinted as Introduction to the Schocken Paperback edition of Tocqueville, 1961.

75. Carl Cohen, *op. cit.*, p. 7.

76. Graham Hughes, *op. cit.*, p. 7.

77. Alexander M. Bickle, as quoted by Hughes, *op. cit.*, p. 10.

78. Court decision in the case of *Baker* v. *Carr*, as quoted by Hughes, *ibid.*, p. 11.

79. To quote Justice James Wilson's early remark (in 1793): "To the

Constitution of the United States the term sovereignty is totally unknown."
80. *Op. cit.*, p. 226.

NOTES

Arendt's own notes for "Civil Disobedience" appear immediately after her essay. The notes below are intended to provide readers with additional guidance. Reference numbers denote page and line of this volume (the line count includes headings). Biblical quotations are keyed to the King James Version. Quotations from Shakespeare are keyed to *The Riverside Shakespeare*, ed. G. Blakemore Evans (Boston: Houghton Mifflin, 1974).

HENRY DAVID THOREAU: CIVIL DISOBEDIENCE

3.2   CIVIL DISOBEDIENCE] First delivered in early 1848 to the Concord Lyceum as two lectures on "the relation of the individual to the State," and originally published in 1849 as "Resistance to Civil Government" in Elizabeth Peabody's periodical *Aesthetic Papers*. It appeared under the title "Civil Disobedience" for the first time in the posthumous collection *A Yankee in Canada, with Anti-Slavery and Reform Papers* (1866), in a version that differs from the *Aesthetic Papers* version in four significant readings, including the title. Since then, the essay has appeared under various titles, among them "On the Duty of Civil Disobedience," the title by which Arendt refers to the essay in her response to Thoreau. The present volume prints the text of "Civil Disobedience" that appeared in *A Yankee in Canada, with Anti-Slavery and Reform Papers* (1866).

6.6   powder-monkeys] Boys employed on ships to carry gun-powder from the powder room to the guns.

6.22–25   "Not a drum . . . we buried."] Charles Wolfe, "The Burial of Sir John Moore at Corunna" (1817).

7.18–19   "stop a hole to keep the wind away,"] Shakespeare, *Hamlet*, V.i.214.

7.21–24   "I am . . . the world."] Shakespeare, *King John*, V.ii.79–82.

8.28–9.11   Paley . . . the other."] William Paley, *The Principles of Moral and Political Philosophy*, 2 vols. (1806). "Resistance to Civil Government," the title under which Thoreau's essay was first published in 1849, is a playful reversal of William Paley's formulation the "duty of *submission* to civil government."

9.25–27   "A drab of state . . . the dirt."] Cyril Tourneur, *The Revenger's Tragedie* (1607), Act V.

21.12–22   Christ answered . . . to know.] See Matthew 22:19–22.

22.16–19   Confucius said . . . of shame."] Thoreau's translation from Jean-Pierre-Guillaume Pauthier, *Confucius et Mencius ou les quatres livres de philosophie moral et politique de la Chine* (Paris: Charpentier, 1841).

30.13   "My Prisons."] Autobiography of Sylvio Pellico (1789–1854), translated into English in 1836.

33.4–9   "We must affect . . . or benefit."] George Peele, *The Battle of Alcazar* (1594), II.ii.425–30.

HANNAH ARENDT: CIVIL DISOBEDIENCE

39.2 CIVIL DISOBEDIENCE] First published in a different form in *The New Yorker*, September 12, 1970; reprinted in *Crises of the Republic* (Harcourt Brace Jovanovich, 1972).

39.15 Eugene V. Rostow] American legal scholar and academic (1913–2002) who served as undersecretary of state for political affairs, 1966–69.

40.3–4 Philip A. Hart's] Legal scholar and politician (1922–1976) who served as a U.S. senator from Michigan, 1959–76.

45.8–9 *in foro conscientiae*] Latin: in the court of conscience; in accordance with moral rather than strictly legal considerations.

53.15 *lumen naturale*] Latin: natural light; innate ability to discern truth.

55.9 "fill a man full of obstacles"] *Richard III*, I.iv.139.

55.13–15 "Conscience is but a word . . . in awe."] *Richard III*, V.iii.309–10.

62.24–28 "'vultures' . . . a barrel"—] Spiro Agnew, address at Pennsylvania Republican Dinner, Harrisburg, October 30, 1969. The vice president's comment followed nationwide protests against the Vietnam War earlier that month.

67.3–4 Marx's admonition to change the world] In his "Theses on Feuerbach" (1888): "The philosophers have only interpreted the world, in various ways. The point is to change it." These words also appear on Marx's tomb.

67.12 *ab ovo*—] Latin: from the egg, the very beginning.

69.11–12 bill recently passed . . . Vietnam war] Passed by both houses of the Massachusetts legislature on April 1, 1970, the Shea

Act, named after its sponsor, H. James Shea of Newton, declared that no inhabitant of the state "shall be required to serve" abroad in an armed conflict in which war has not been declared by Congress, under Article I, Section 8, clause 11, of the Constitution.

72.24   *constitutio libertatis*] Latin: the constitution of freedom. In *On Revolution*, Chapter Four: Foundation I: *Constitutio Libertatis*, Arendt writes: "Clearly the true objective of the American Constitution was not to limit power but to create more power, actually establish and duly constitute an entirely new power centre, destined to compensate the confederate republic, whose authority was to be exerted over a large, expanding territory, for the power lost through the separation of the colonies from the English crown. . . . The American Constitution finally consolidated the power of the Revolution, and since the aim of revolution was freedom, it indeed came to be . . . *Constitutio Libertatis*, the foundation of freedom."

74.26–27   as John Cotton rightly remarked . . . best form of government."] In a letter to Lord Saye and Sele, written in 1636.

85.13   Babbitts] George F. Babbitt, character in Sinclair Lewis's novel *Babbitt* (1922), whose name is synonymous with American middle-class values and complacency.

88.2   *pacta sunt servanda*—] Latin: agreements must be kept.

91.7–8   *inter arma silent leges*] Latin: amidst arms, laws are silent.

About the Authors

HANNAH ARENDT was born on October 14, 1906, in a borough of Hanover, Germany, the only child of politically progressive and secular Jewish parents. At the University of Marburg, she studied philosophy under Martin Heidegger, whose thinking would exert a notable influence on her later work. Following her year at Marburg, she spent a semester at the University of Freiburg, before moving on to the University of Heidelberg, where in 1928 she earned a doctorate in philosophy at age twenty-two. Her dissertation on Augustine's concept of *caritas* (neighborly love) was written under the direction of Karl Jaspers. After Adolf Hitler came to power in 1933, Arendt, having been arrested briefly for illegal research into anti-Semitism, fled Nazi Germany and emigrated to Paris. In 1940, once again in flight from the Nazis, she left France and made her way to the United States by way of Portugal. In 1941, Arendt settled in New York, her primary residence for the remainder of her life, where she became part of an intellectual circle that included Mary McCarthy, Dwight Macdonald, Alfred Kazin, Lionel Trilling, and Delmore Schwartz. Arendt taught at various American universities, including Princeton, the University of Chicago, and The New School for Social Research. Her major works of political thought were written after she became a naturalized U.S. citizen in 1950. In 1951, she published *The Origins of Totalitarianism*, a study of Nazi Germany and Stalinist Russia, followed in 1958 by *The Human Condition*, which offered a narrative of the modern age told through the human activities of labor, work, and action. Arendt also published a steady stream of literary and biographical essays and political journalism. Her best-known book, *Eichmann in Jerusalem* (1963, rev. 1964)—a portrait of Adolf Eichmann, a leading administrator of the Holocaust—came out of a series of articles written for *The New Yorker*. Her influential historical study *On Revolution* (1963) offered a comparative estimate of the American and French Revolutions. At the time of her death on December 4, 1975, of a heart attack, she was at work on a three-volume study, *The Life of the Mind*, on the faculties of thinking, willing, and judging.

HENRY DAVID THOREAU was born on July 12, 1817, in Concord, Massachusetts, into a family that was frequently in difficult financial straits until the 1850s. His father worked successively as a farmer, grocer, teacher, and manufacturer of pencils. After attending Concord Academy, Thoreau studied at Harvard College from 1833 to 1837, taking courses in rhetoric, classics,

German, philosophy, and science. The young Thoreau formed a close relationship with Ralph Waldo Emerson, who had moved to Concord in 1834, and through him with others associated with the Transcendentalist group, including Margaret Fuller, Bronson Alcott, Jones Very, and Theodore Parker. He worked in his father's pencil factory while embarking on a journal that eventually ran to over two million words. With his brother, John, he ran Concord Academy, from 1831 to 1841, teaching foreign languages and science. He published poems and essays in *The Dial* (which he helped edit), beginning with the first issue in July 1840. He became an intimate friend and frequent companion of William Ellery Channing, the poet and nephew of the Unitarian minister of the same name. In 1845, Thoreau built a cabin on Emerson's property at Walden Pond, where he stayed for a little over two years while continuing to lead an active social life. In an act of civil disobedience, he spent a night in jail in 1846 for nonpayment of poll tax (which he believed supported the institution of slavery and the U.S. invasion and occupation of Mexico). His first book, *A Week on the Concord and Merrimack Rivers* (1849), most of it written at Walden Pond, was based on a boat trip made in 1839 with his brother, John, who died in 1842 of lockjaw. In the 1850s, he supported himself as a surveyor and continued to work in the family business, now supplying ground lead for electrotyping. *Walden*, on which he had worked since his residence at the pond, went through multiple revisions before its publication in 1854. Thoreau met John Brown in 1857, and following Brown's Harpers Ferry raid delivered "A Plea for John Brown in Concord, Boston, and Worcester. He worked for many years on a projected study of American Indians, compiling thousands of pages of notes and extracts. He died on May 6, 1862, of tuberculosis. *The Maine Woods* (1864) and *Cape Cod* (1865) were published posthumously.

This book is set in 10½ point Minion Pro, a digital typeface designed by American typographer Robert Slimbach in 1990 for Adobe Systems and inspired by Renaissance-era fonts. The name comes from the traditional nomenclature for type sizes, the smallest of which was diamond, followed by pearl, agate, nonpareil, minion, brevier, bourgeois, long primer, small pica, pica, etc. The display type is a new sans serif font, Praktika, released in 2017 by Finnish designer and illustrator Emil Bertell and modeled after the early-twentieth-century grotesque typefaces used in European road signs.

The paper is acid-free and exceeds the requirements for permanence established by the American National Standards Institute.

Text design and composition by Gopa & Ted2, Inc., Albuquerque, NM.
Printing and binding by Sheridan, Saline, MI.